Legal Theory Today
Law and Aesthetics

Legal Theory Today

General Editor

John Gardner, Professor of Jurisprudence, University College, Oxford

TITLES IN THIS SERIES

Law and Aesthetics

Adam Gearey

General Editor: John Gardner

·HART·
PUBLISHING

OXFORD – PORTLAND OREGON
2001

Hart Publishing
Oxford and Portland, Oregon

Published in North America (US and Canada) by
Hart Publishing
c/o International Specialized Book Services
5804 NE Hassalo Street
Portland, Oregon
97213-3644
USA

Distributed in the Netherlands, Belgium and Luxembourg
by
Intersentia, Churchillaan 108
B2900 Schoten
Antwerpen
Belgium

Hart Publishing is a specialist legal publisher based in Oxford,
England.
To order further copies of this book or to request a list of other
publications please write to:

Hart Publishing, Salter's Boatyard, Folly Bridge,
Abingdon Road, Oxford OX1 4LB
Telephone: +44 (0)1865 245533 or Fax: +44 (0)1865 794882
e-mail: mail@hartpub.co.uk
WEBSITE: http//:www.hartpub.co.uk

British Library Cataloguing in Publication Data
Data Available
ISBN 1–84113–243–8 (hardback)
1–84113–026–5 (paperback)

Typeset by Hope Services (Abingdon) Ltd.
Printed and bound in Great Britain by
Lightning Source UK Ltd

Acknowledgements

I read somewhere that a book always carries with it the souls of the writer's friends and those who contributed to its coming into the world. There is quite a crowd between the pages of this volume. John Gardner read the manuscript countless times and made me work to defend what I had written. I would like to thank him for his insight and his help. Julie Dickson provided a most perspicuous and encouraging commentary on a final draft. Richard Hart's help and encouragement was also deeply appreciated. Conversations in the Harringay Arms with Mike Meehan helped to clarify difficult questions of poetry with Courage and wit. Thanos Zaratoulidis' calm wisdom was of immense importance, as was his help with the Greek. Nathan Moore brought Deleuzian insight into matters of force and flux. Alexander Carnera Ljungsrom explicated the joyous science in masterly fashion on a fine day in London under wide, blue skies. Patrick Hanafin, Piyel Haldar, Maria Drakopoulou, Les Moran, Sue Baines, Eleanor Loizidou, Tatiana Flessas, Valerie Hoare, Emma Sandon, Helen Reece, Peter Fitzpatrick, Maria Aristodemou and Patricia Tuit assisted the resolution of difficult questions in cultural studies, feminism, communism, appearances and disappearances, genealogy, queer theory and race theory. My thanks go also to Costas Douzinas and Peter Goodrich, the Jagger and Richards of postmodern legal theory. Costas Douzinas read an earlier draft of the manuscript and gave me hope; Peter Goodrich provided inspiration from abroad. Pannu Minkinnen made useful and insightful comments on what became Chapter 2.

A version of the final chapter was read at the Critical Legal Conference 2000 in Helsinki, and benefited greatly from the contributions of Kaisa Makela, Toomas Kotkas, Barry Collins and Ari Hirvonen. This book also owes a lot to a conversation with Robert Cartledge in Morfa Nefyn on the night of the meteorite storm and on many occasions since.

This book is for Mary Gearey, with my love and thanks.

ADAM GEAREY
London
November 2000.

General Editor's Preface

By its nature, law makes moral claims. But can it be judged only by moral standards? Clearly not. It can also be regarded and evaluated as, among other things, an object of aesthetic appreciation: as a literary genre, an intellectual architecture, a social spectacle, and so on. Lawyers not infrequently come to think of their work as one might think of a work of art, prizing elegance, coherence, balance, and other aesthetic virtues, over moral virtues such as honesty, generosity, and humanity. Even justice —the one moral virtue which lawyers find it hard to avoid mentioning—is transformed by some legal thinkers into an aesthetic form. Never mind sensitivity to people's needs and predicaments, just look at that symmetry, that order!

This prizing of the aesthetic over the moral—or of form over substance, as the point is often (misleadingly) put—may strike one as the most extreme case of lawyers' narcissism. Not suprisingly this very accusation was one of the original inspirations behind the critical legal studies movement, whose members saw in the elegant conceits of what they called "legal formalism" a kind of unhealthy escapism from "the field of pain and death" (as Robert Cover put it) in which law operates. And yet some critical legal studies writers merely compounded the felony with a new version of the same narcissism. They became the *enfants terribles* of the law school, replacing the formalists' passion for finding coherence and order in the law with a like passion for finding incoherence and disorder. Many were subversives only in the way that the dadaists and the absurdists were subversives. They subverted the values of the traditional legal aesthetes but in the process they reinforced the view that law is mainly an object of aesthetic criticism, mainly suited to being deconstructed and transfigured and problematized. Their work stood to the "formalism" of some lawyers as a Hirst sheep in formaldehyde stands to a Constable landscape. Our preconceptions were challenged but still we seemed to be stuck in a virtual moral vacuum. Only the blandest and most naive moral truisms (look, people are still being oppressed!) lurked behind the sophisticated countercultural manoeuvres.

So the question arises: Is there any authentic moral insight lurking within an aesthetics of law? Does approaching the law as an object of aesthetic appreciation count as any more than a vain distraction from the real job of revealing its moral strengths and weaknesses? Adam Gearey's book tackles these problems by gradually drawing us into the web of Nietzsche's revisionist aesthetic morality, in which the highest admiration is reserved for the testing of one's creative limits, and in which true virtue lies in overcoming all that constrains and dampens the human spirit. You may think it curious to talk—it is my expression, not Gearey's—of Nietzsche's "aesthetic morality". Wasn't Nietzsche's aim to put morality behind us altogether? Well, yes and no. Nietzsche always read the word "morality" to mean "what people conventionally take to be morally required of them", and this cod-morality understandably appalled him. But what he wanted to see in its place was first and foremost a better set of moral judgments, with various traits conventionally classified as moral weaknesses reclassified as moral strengths, and vice versa. One of Nietzsche's fancies was that in this rival vision of human flourishing, the true values of ethics and aesthetics would converge. By the subversion of the conventional, the human spirit would have its beauty, as well as its honour, restored. It is from this aspect of the Nietzschean dream that Adam Gearey takes his cue. A Nietzchean legal aesthetics—a full appreciation of law's creative potential—is also a new morality of law.

The voice of the book that follows—as you can tell from this trailer—is relentlessly optimistic, and the dream Nietzsche prevails over his nightmare counterpart. The nightmare counterpart is of course the Nietzsche for whom "creative potential" includes the potential to murder and destroy, for whom just thinking the conventionally unthinkable—however monstrous—is an act of liberation for the human spirit. With that nightmare in mind, one may be tempted to conclude that we still need to distinguish *within* our creativity between good and evil uses of it, and that an aesthetics of law ordered around creativity must in that respect still be answerable to a relatively independent ethics of law. But there speaks the pessimist, for whom the human power to create includes the power to create misery as readily as joy. This work is by and large an imaginative celebration of the opposite view. I must say that in that respect I found it exhilerating and indeed liberating, and hence a nice exemplification of its own thesis. By the same token it is the most stylistically *outré* of the books published so far in the *Legal Theory Today* series, for in true Nietzschean spirit it is as literary as it is philosophical. In abandoning old hostilities and building intriguing new bridges, however, it clearly belongs with the other books. It is the work of a generous spirit as well as a sparkling wit, and to that extent moral and aesthetic virtues do indeed converge within its pages.

John Gardner
University College, Oxford
14 May 2001

Contents

1
Ozymandias

If understanding law as an aesthetic phenomenon requires the
insights of poets and philosophers, the best approach presents
itself as a poetic philosophy.

What follows are notes towards a possible aesthetics of law.

To say anything meaningful about art one makes an explicit
or implicit reference to rules and standards. For instance, to distinguish between a poem and a novel or to invoke criteria of aesthetic worth, one must refer to rules of genre, and standards of
excellence. It may be that aesthetics can cast light on law's rule-
based nature. Although there are clearly differences between the
two subjects, an intriguing overlap could be defined. Indeed, it
might be thought that the artist is like the lawyer, in that both
have a working knowledge of rules. Their product, art or legal
argument, represents a mature understanding of the ways in
which they are constrained and the opportunities to be creative.
This approach is comforting. It supports the lawyer's desire for
order, confirming the prejudice that law arranges the world in
the best possible way, and that he or she is a creative individual.

However, there is something disturbing in comparing law and
art. The artist's fear that over-analysis, over-reduction to rules,
will destroy the aesthetic experience suggests that there is more
to art than rules. Inspiration, the creative force, cannot be cap-
tured and codified. There is another objection: why should the
law begin to describe itself as an aesthetics, to draw yet another
aspect of social life into its rage for order?

Should aesthetics become an elaboration of the order and
operation of the law or should it sketch a more problematic and
disturbing relationship? This book will propose the latter course.
Exemplifying different aspects of the first approach will be the

work of Ernest J. Weinrib and James Boyd White. Weinrib shows how an understanding of law's formal beauty can illuminate the subject's coherence, identity and place in the social world. These ideas will criticised for employing an unduly restrictive notion of the aesthetic. White, on the other hand, presents law as a form of conversation, an understanding different from Weinrib's tightly defined idea of legal structure. White deploys an idea of aesthetic reasoning exemplified by literary criticism to give insights into legal discourse. He argues that the aesthetic nature of legal reasoning allows it to balance and reconcile conflicting claims. This work will also be criticised. It plays down the disruptive nature of aesthetics and ignores a kind of poetry that would show the unsure foundations on which modern law is constructed. Elaborating this argument means concentrating on an alternative understanding of law and aesthetics that can be found in the work of Percy Bysshe Shelley.

An education in aesthetics: Weinrib and aesthetic formalism

Some fear that law is losing touch with the world it is meant to order. Its strict categories and rigours of argument serve to rigidify its ability to respond to the social world. One way of defending the law is to invoke the aesthetic. Indeed, the work that is to be studied in the first two sections of this chapter could be understood as providing lawyers with an aesthetic education.[1] Using aesthetic ideas to explain the law shows that law is not a harsh, inflexible science; it is an art.

Weinrib's aesthetics work within some carefully drawn parameters that have to be outlined. Theory has to respect the specific nature of law. Recent developments in legal thought have obscured this truth. Weinrib asserts that a marked feature of contemporary scholarship is an uncertainty or even a celebration of the permeability of traditional subject boundaries.

[1] For an explanation of this term and its derivation from Friedrich Schiller's *On the Aesthetic Education of Man*, see Meszaros, I., *Marx's Theory of Alienation* (London, Merlin Press, 1978), ch. X.

One of the major culprits is functionalist scholarship. Functionalism, as expressed in both legal realism and in law and economics scholarship, commits a serious error in conceiving of law as reflecting a certain set of policy goals. Thus, legal realism tended to resort to sociology or psychology to explain how the law operates. Law and economics scholarship, as its name suggests, discovers the relevance of economic explanations. Weinrib's objection is that this work imports concepts from other disciplines that cannot properly account for the operation of purely legal concepts.[2]

Legal aesthetics must not fall into error. Weinrib argues that law embodies a sense of beauty informed by ideas of proportion and coherent development. The work of the literary critic Northrop Frye is used to elaborate this idea of form: ' "Every poem must necessarily be a unity,' says Blake: this, as the wording implies, is not a statement of fact about all existing poems, but a statement of the hypothesis which every reader adopts in first trying to comprehend the most chaotic poem ever written.'[3]

[2] Weinrib accuses cross-disciplinary scholarship of a serious methodological error: infinite regress. If a subject can be understood only by reference to another subject, then the subject of reference must, likewise, be explicable by reference to another subject, a process that becomes one of perpetual deferral of the 'truth'. This argument is not convincing. The claims made by cross-disciplinary scholars do not necessarily demand that one subject is explained by another subject in an open-ended way. For instance, a scholar in law and economics may claim that law is at root understandable only by economic concepts that are more fundamental than legal concepts. This is not a deferral of the truth of law. It is a claim about what constitutes law's identity. Even if the infinite regress argument fails, it could still be maintained that cross-disciplinary approaches impose concerns on legal study that are alien to law's internal dynamic. This belief in law's autonomy would depend on there being a legal nature that could be identified and distinguished from other disciplines. There are disagreements within legal scholarship about whether this line can be held. The danger is that law and aesthetics dissolve the specificity of law. Later in this chapter, it will be argued that this fear is, to some degree, realised, but in a way that is not directly anticipated by either the defenders or the detractors of cross-disciplinary work.

[3] Weinrib, E.J., *The Idea of Private Law* (Cambridge, Mass., Harvard University Press, 1995), 43. For a different application of Frye's work to legal theory, see West, R., 'Jurisprudence as Narrative: An Aesthetic Analysis of Modern Legal Theory' (1985) 60 *New York University Law Review* 145. West

The lesson formalism learns from literature is the necessity of form. Even works that deny form must utilise it to the extent that their particular deviations can be understood. Consider James Joyce's *Finnegans Wake*. To engage with the book one has to presuppose that there are novelistic conventions that operate at an ideal level, because otherwise Joyce's experiments would make no sense at all (although the possibility remains that *Finnegans Wake* makes no sense at all). Thus, at the heart of literary or legal formalism is a belief in the inherent worth of form. Form bestows identity and coherence on the phenomenon of study. The idea of form is a prerequisite to the study of any discipline. Form enables the positing of an entity apart from the primal disorder that precedes identity; form describes a phenomenon's singularity and specificity. In jurisprudence, formalism describes an approach that seeks to isolate and classify law's unique organising principles.

Weinrib's contention is that private laws provide the most exemplary articulation of law's form. Law's distinctive nature has to be found in what is most true to it: its origin. The core of law's being is pure and unadulterated by any extrinsic considerations. This quest for the origin is scholarship as a clearing of distraction and debris, to allow a revelation of law's foundations. Formalism discovers first principles in the resolution of a dispute between two private individuals, a plaintiff and a defendant. Central concepts, such as harm, duty, right and causation, are the grammar used to articulate this relationship as a fundamental point of reference that can account for law at both a procedural and doctrinal level.

Law's articulation and resolution of liability reveal the perfect beauty of the underlying principles of reason. In other words, legal

uses Frye's notion of narrative archetypes to classify contemporary jurisprudence. If this were to be read against Weinrib's coherence thesis, it might suggest that there is a correspondence between legal theory and other disciplines. Law is encoded by narrative archetypes because these archetypes reveal universal truths about the human condition. Interestingly, Frye's work can thus be used to very different ends, supporting both a notion of law's formal autonomy and a theory of law's similarity to other disciplines.

decisions are not merely the expressions of state power or determination of cases on an individual basis. Law is a structure of reasoned argument. Its inherent rationality is shown by its tendency to coherence. Legal argument avoids contradiction and indeterminacy and endeavours to manifest a 'harmony' of its principles and rules. That this structure should be described in a metaphor drawn from music again indicates the aesthetic ballast of this argument. When a lawyer looks into the law, he or she finds the perfect form of the discipline: connections of rules and principles elaborated from a central idea. These are the assumptions that the community of legal interpreters share. If one does not accept this position, one is simply not licensed to enter into legal argument.

Coherence is central to justification in rational terms. Law has to provide justifications for its decisions, and an argument that does not cohere with the wider structure is likely to be a less persuasive and a weaker justification than an argument that appears to 'fit' with the wider discourse. It would be wrong, however, to overstate this coherence of law. Incoherent decisions can be made. Coherence maintains, however, that the process is self-correcting. Erroneous decisions detracting from the logic of the structure will ultimately be identified and corrected. Coherence as 'intelligibility' suggests, in the final instance, that law is a unity. This unity is achieved by the structure having no external reference.[4] Intelligibility is achieved internally through the coherent relationship of the parts to the whole.

Formalism has an 'immanent moral rationality'.[5] Private law as a form of 'moral association'[6] supposes that its norms can be used in an argument any rational being would find compelling in instances of dispute. To retain their moral authority, legal arguments must make reference to the intrinsic ordering of the discourse. Consider a hypothetical tort case. It would have to be resolved by reference to the culpability of the plaintiff, defined through such terms as the existence of a duty of care and a causation chain that linked the defendant's negligent act to the

[4] Weinrib, E.J., *supra* n. 3, 14.
[5] *Ibid.*, 23.
[6] *Ibid.*, 39.

plaintiff's harm. To be consistent and justificatory, a legal argument could not make reference to ideas such as the spreading of costs for accidents on principles that do not privilege the culpability of the defendant. Introducing such considerations would be arbitrary, as it would introduce terms that do not fall within the argumentative ordering of the law.

The wider framework of this image of justice rests on borrowings from Kant. Kant's philosophy is favoured, in part, for its aesthetic qualities. It is the 'prism' that 'diffuses' practical reason into the form of law.[7] Kant's 'idea of reason' provides the controlling concept that allows a rational jurisprudence to account for the origins of civil society without reference to anything extrinsic to reason itself. In this sense it provides a further justification for Weinrib's own vision of law's formal beauty; indeed, it allows a linkage between a formal idea of law and a wider theory of society. Thus for Kant, the social contract defines the point when freedom in the state of nature is exchanged for the protection of a 'lawful commonwealth'. This contract is neither a fact of history nor necessarily a way of preventing, internecine violence. Its relevance is, rather, that it is presupposed by rational organisation. Requirements of rational organisation, in turn, oblige the legislator to frame laws as if they represented the general will, and to proceed on the basis that rational citizens would consent to laws that embodied the general will.[8]

What is wrong with Weinrib's vision of aesthetics?

Although Weinrib wants to reveal the truth of the law, the narrowness of his categories makes his argument unconvincing. Law appears no more than a grand ideal, a glittering structure removed from the compromises of the world. Ironically, despite the caveats about the risks of borrowing from other disciplines obscuring the nature of the object, it may be the case that this account moves too far in the opposite direction. Law becomes

[7] Weinrib, E.J., *supra* n. 3, 100.
[8] *Ibid.*, 86.

too aesthetic; like a particularly beautiful picture or sculpture, it needs to be preserved from the ravages of the world and time. If reason is a formal principle, if art can remind us of this, then history becomes close to irrelevant. We have fallen away from a time when the law was whole, when reason and law were a unity. All we have to do is to return to a truth that Weinrib's work discovers and preserves. The use of Kant's social contract runs up against similar problems. Law must deal with ahistorical general forms. It can have no proper consideration of the specific problems of embodied people of different races and genders, as it always refers to an overarching idea that difference can be reduced to similitude.[9]

The cost of saving the law is to strip it down to what are perceived as its essentials. Law exists as an algebraic sign, denuded of content in the name of the system's immaculateness and universal relevance. Should aesthetics lead to such a closed model of the law? Although Weinrib makes use of aesthetic arguments, there is no real probing of the possibilities of aesthetic forms other than formalism. For instance, modernist aesthetics shows the interconnection of different discourses[10] and allows an imaginative engagement with economics and politics. Formalism's narrow focus makes it difficult to account for the influence of these 'extrinsic' factors. From Weinrib's perspective, consideration of such elements would be a dangerous loss of focus from the articulation of specifically legal principles. Ultimately, then, aesthetic considerations are overdetermined by a requirement for law's purity. This application of the aesthetic produces a very closed model of the law. In turning to White's work, one discovers a more 'open'-textured presentation of law's aesthetic nature that perhaps provides a more dynamic idea of legal aesthetics,

---

[9] Consider, for example, the discussion of feminist, critical race and 'queer' scholarship in Ch. 4.

[10] This could be demonstrated by brief reference to the aesthetics of Ezra Pound's *Cantos*. The *Cantos* bring together, amongst other concerns, economic theory, Confucian philosophy, American, Asian and European history and various mythologies.

but which still does not contend with the real challenges posed by an aesthetics of law.

The consolations of poetry: the aesthetics of James Boyd White

James Boyd White challenges the closure of formalism whilst stressing a need to maintain a sense of law's distinctive coherence. His starting point is a contention that law is inseparable from other forms of life and other disciplines. Law is a language, and language is inherently part of the social world. As any particular use of language takes place against a background of assumptions about shared meaning conventions that allow the individual speaker to construct sentences that will be understood, the varieties of language have to be classified.[11] Law has to be seen as ' a culture of argument', a distinctive set of practices and ways of interacting in the world. Law's defining concern is with texts of authority, and the arguments that can be developed from these texts to resolve disputes. Law is rhetoric. It is an 'art of persuasion' and 'deliberation', a search for authoritative solutions in the midst of disagreement. Law as a constitutive rhetoric 'creates' actors and conventions that enable the creation of arguments.[12]

[11] White, J.B., *Justice as Translation* (Chicago, Ill., University of Chicago Press, 1990), p. xiii.

[12] For an exemplification of this process, consider White's reading of the Federalist Papers, *supra* n.11, 45. The first of the Federalist Papers calls upon those present to 'deliberate'. This opening sentence is a kind of 'promise' that exists between the text and the reader to co-operate in the performance of its central claims. The forcefulness of this introduction is a performance of what the reader can expect; the statement of passionately held beliefs in an argumentative forum that presupposes dialogue and debate. Of course there will be bias, but the voice behind the Federalist Papers is capable of balanced self-reflection. To participate in this foundation of good government, one has to be ready to engage in a form of discourse. Deliberation is itself the very underpinning of the community imagined by the text. To remain true to this call, the reader has to be alive to essentially literary concerns. The rationality that underlies this text knows that terms cannot be defined. Meaning is yet to come.

This location of law appears more promising. Insisting on a degree of autonomy means that the law does not become closed in upon itself. Furthermore, it allows law to be saved from a particularly contemporary problem. Discourses proliferate, each with their own paradigms and practices. The sense of any meaningful whole, any coherent organisation of knowledge is lost. Would it be possible to reintegrate 'reason' and 'emotion', science and ethics? White regrets that it is no longer possible to make a normative claim that is seen as a rational and compelling statement rather than an unjustifiable imposition of a more powerful view. He is aware that although the use of the word 'integration' is suspect, the term can be redefined and become useful to legal theory. Redefinition would play down the connotations of some form of ultimate unity, with all the implicit reference to a master language that this entails. Integration can be defined as toleration for difference. To further these arguments, White turns to a model of literary composition. The literary work brings together different elements in a form that can preserve their meanings and not reduce them to a single term. When we encounter this mode of combination, it works a transformation on us. We appreciate the creation of a new 'thing' in the world that suggests unforeseen possibilities. This mode of meaning creation is exemplified by poetry.

Literature is imagined as a discourse that can repair the ruptures of thought. The skill called for is the ability to obtain a perspective on different positions without merging them, balancing and integrating various claims. This process is best exemplified in the development of a literary sensibility honed on the close reading of classic literature. To develop this position and offer a criticism of it, it is necessary to focus on a particular poem and the claims that can be made about the reading process. White uses Robert Frost's *A Dust of Snow*:

The way a crow
Shook down on me
The dust of snow
From a hemlock tree

> Has given my heart
> A change of mood
> And saved some part
> Of a day I had rued.[13]

White's reading performs an instructive move from a sense of dislocation and cultural pessimism to a realisation of new possibilities. A close textual study of the poem shows that it works by playing two simultaneous levels of meaning off against each other. At the most basic level the poem's narrative tells of a walk in the woods, and the poet's surprise at seeing a crow in a tree that shakes snow upon him. The crow is sat in a 'hemlock tree'.

Symbolically, the associations here are with death, perhaps more particularly with the death of Socrates. Despite the sadness, though, the surprise of the chance encounter gives the poet a 'change of mood'. In a symbolic register, this can be associated with 'grace' and 'redemption'.[14] The poem, then, does not allow the symbolic level to overcome the details that read as simple observations of the world. It effectively integrates them into a 'whole', a complex structure of meaning that allows us to read the two levels at the same time, to be aware of their difference, and how they contribute equally to the overall effect of the poem. In reading the poem, one becomes aware that it cannot be reduced to a paraphrase. It delivers no 'message,' there is no single 'view' behind it. Rather, the reader has to approach it sensitive to its ambiguities.[15]

White's practice operates with a very definite model of literary meaning. To challenge the viability of his vision of literature would have shock effects that spread through the whole territory. Can Frost's poem display a different operation of language to that described by White?

[13] White, n. 11 *supra*, 5

[14] *Ibid.*, 6.

[15] White's sensitivity to the melancholy that pervades the poem is possibly triggered by what is at stake in his own project. If his reading shows that the darkness of the poem can be moved towards some measure of light, it will suggest that any literary text can ultimately exemplify the project of the cultural renewal that White recommends.

Although White's reading can, to some extent, celebrate the poem's ambiguous language it appears that at the end of this reading session, a scaffold of meaning has been built around the piece. But the poem resists such an imposition of meaning. It is necessary to return to the idea that the poem witnesses the strangeness of a peculiar event that breaks out of a routine. There is a tension between the form, that attempts to capture the experience, and the experience itself. It would be possible to play off, then, the regularity of the form, the four-line stanzas with the ABAB rhyme with the symbolism of the shock that the 'dust' of snow provides. 'Dust' can of course be read as suggesting at one level death, the reading that White chooses, but in this reading it could suggest a strange, diaphanous and formless property that disappears from the poem like the event it signifies. There is a further symbolic and semantic association to the colour of the snow and the crow that will be explored presently. To remain true to White's close reading, the syntax of the poem and its relation to the imagery need to be briefly examined.

Structurally, this poem is one sentence extended over two stanzas. Separating the stanzas is the white space of the page. This effects a suspension of meaning when the reader comes to the end of the first stanza. The sentence begins in the first stanza, is interrupted, and concludes in the second stanza. The whiteness of the dust of the snow can be related to this interrupting gap at the poem's centre. This is the space of surprise at the heart of the piece. The rhyme snow/crow contrasts the colours and their symbolic associations, but in a way that White might resist. It is a pun, perhaps even a pun on White's own name: no reading is black and white, open and shut. The surprising dust of snow that is given meaning by the poem returns to formlessness. No reading can determine its meaning. Why? Because this poem does not want to be read. Reading remains between the black and the white, the letters, the lines, the punctuation, and the spaces that will forever suspend what these signifying marks might like to convey. This impossible space is also the space of the reader, and the poem falls in front of the reader like the dust of snow from the tree.

The reading above is not meant to be flippant or confusing. It is an attempt to demonstrate that White's literary practice does not capture a meaning from a poem that wants to retain its mysteriousness. The next move in this critique is to link this point about literary language to a wider normative theory about the nature of literary language.

Practical criticism, White asserts, is a way of reading alive to the ethical and moral dimensions of the text under study. As an aesthetics, practical criticism was always an ethical endeavor. Literary education was a rigorous practice that asked a reader to weigh up a text within the terms of his or her own experience. Borrowing these techniques and using them in law do mean modification. A lawyer is constrained differently from a literary critic. In both literature and law, however, the critic or the lawyer is attempting to keep a text alive. Whether making an argument before a judge or arguing about the meaning of a poem, the interpreter is negotiating claims of authority and presenting the meaning of a text in a form for others to judge.

Legal judgment is the 'art' of the 'reconstitution' of texts.[16] Law thus takes part in the general forms of cultural life in as much as it preserves the meanings and importance of historical texts. Texts of authority are constantly placed in new contexts and their claims and doctrines weighed up in the light of present demands. But it is not just that law preserves and reinterprets authoritative texts. There is also a question of how the reading of texts takes place. White's guiding thread in following this process is a quotation from John Dewey: 'Democracy begins in conversation'.[17] Conversations presuppose interlocutors, and an exchange between people who respect the views and authority of those with whom they are talking. Legal argument does not simply make dictatorial claims that should be obeyed, it is an occasion for reasoned discussion about the authority of the text in question. If one approaches a legal judgment with this in

---

[16] White, n. 11 *supra*, 99.
[17] *Ibid.*, 91.

mind, one's attention becomes focused on the argument as much as the result in itself. This is to say that although the judgment represents in one way the result of a case, it is in itself a text and has to be approached in a 'radically literary' manner.

The radical literary reading of the law is an attempt to connect an aesthetics with an ethics. White argues for an understanding of pluralism, an 'other-orientated' theory of literary communication. Community is the essential negotiation of competing claims to meaning that are immanent to communication. Literature is privileged as it allows an appreciation of the way the world is constructed through words:

> Every text is written in a language, and that language always entails commitments to views of the world, of oneself, of one's readers, and of others with which the writer must somehow come to terms. Similarly, every text is radically social: it always defines a speaker, an audience, and a relation between them, and it may define others as well, as potential readers or as objects of that discourse. Every text thus creates a community, and it is responsible for the community it creates.[18]

The notion of 'translation' developed as a model of justice has this idea of a community of interpretation at its base. Translation is an acknowledgement of the necessary dialogue that a text generates. Whereas legal discourse seeks to map out and define an area through logic and to hold to universal truth claims:

> [T]he literary method, on the other hand, knows that nothing can be said with certain truth or validity, that no one can be compelled to submit, and that submission is worthless any way. It proceeds on the assumption that our categories and terms are perpetually losing and acquiring meaning; that they mean different things to different people and in different texts. It is not a territorial claim but an invitation to reflection.[19]

[18] White, J.B., 'Law and Literature: No Manifesto' (1988) *Mercer Law Review* 739ff.

[19] White, n. 11 *supra*, 42.

The literary becomes the privileged trope for thinking the ethics behind the notion of translation. Translation respects the 'other' as the source of meaning, as the originator of a text that comes from a source other than the self. It is a respect for this otherness that characterises good translation that does not seek to reduce the other to a set of common terms, but to preserve the original difference. The notion of the inherently ethical nature of translation moves beyond the notion of the literary text, and becomes a model of conversation, a form of discourse ethics. Social relationships can be thought of as involving a conversation, where each side has to respect the other. Absolute understanding is not possible, or even desirable; what is necessary is the fidelity to the conversation, the need to translate and respond to the terms of the other.

White's argument that literary language is ethical is not convincing. Consider the counter-reading of *A Dust of Snow*. How could the ethically orientated nature of this poem be described? If anything, the poem seems irresponsible. It appears to be playing a rather unfair game with the reader, refusing to reveal what it appears to know. This kind of chicanery would be an unsure foundation for any ethics. This is not to say that there could not be a way of linking ethics to aesthetics, an alternative will be elaborated in Chapter 3. However, may it suffice to suggest for the moment that, even within understandings of literary language, the idea that it can be linked to an honest attitude towards others is difficult. To offer an illustrative quotation, which is not meant to settle the argument but to suggest at least one authoritative disagreement to White, it may be useful to refer to Auden's elegy for Yeats.[20] Time forgives the writers' faults, even pardoning the fascist poet Paul Claudel and Kipling's imperialism, not for any ethical reasons, but simply for 'writing well'. Writing, then, and the criteria of literary success are not necessarily related to ethical matters.

[20] Auden, W.H., *In Memoriam W.B. Yeats:* 'Time that with this strange excuse/pardons Kipling and his views,/And will pardon Paul Claudel,/Pardons him for writing well': in Mendelson, E. (ed.), *W.H. Auden Selected Poems* (London, Faber and Faber, 1979), 80.

A dust of sand

It is easy to misread Shelley's *A Defence of Poetry* and to turn it into a variation on White's literary jurisprudence. Consider the famous statement that poets are the unacknowledged legislators of the world.[21] It appears to make a universal claim about some form of law that applies to all men and women. White's work might suggest that this is the law of language that connects to self and others. Poetic language acts morally on the hearer. It serves to supplement the calculations of reason and to deny the baser desires, allowing the individual to imagine himself in the place of others. Poetry encourages a moral imagination that adds spirit to the dry classifications of ethical science.[22] Shelley would appear to support the argument that practical criticism is an inherently flexible act of reading that does not seek to formalise like science, but to negotiate and balance competing claims.

However, as we read on, these arguments cannot be supported with such facility. Although poetry is 'moral' it does not appear to have a content. Shelley states that 'a poet . . . would do ill to embody his own conception of right and wrong, which are usually those of his place and time, in his poetical creations, which participate in neither'.[23] It would seem, then, that the 'morality' that underlies the law for Shelley indicates what cannot be definitively named. Morality could not be described, for instance, as a democratic conversation. Poetry escapes a determinate moral content because poets are prophets, 'unacknowledged legislators'[24] who address futurity. Futurity, the time of things that are to come, is open. The future cannot be foretold. Shelley is keen to stress that it is in this sense that poets are correctly called prophets, prophets who cannot foretell, but who welcome the future. These prophets seem strange legislators. It is hard to know exactly what it is that their laws might promulgate. What, then, is the work of the poet?

[21] Shelley P.B., 'A Defence of Poetry' in Shawcross, J. (ed.), *Shelley's Literary and Philosophical Criticism* (London, Henry Frowde, 1909), 131.

[22] *Ibid.*, 131.

[23] *Ibid.*,132.

[24] *Ibid.*, 159.

The poet's imagination is a dying ember fanned by the breath of inspiration. This is an important metaphor. Earlier in the piece, the distinction between reason and imagination had allowed Shelley to posit a separation between analytical science and the synthetic quality of imagination. The latter term was then privileged in a definition of poetry. However, this polarity becomes disturbed. A third term enters the definition. Poetry brings something back from divine regions, from the nether spaces of the non-human. This return challenges both synthetic and analytical powers of the mind. It does not respond to the will. A poet cannot simply decide to write. What is worse, the very act of composition signifies that the spirit of imagination has been and gone. Even the greatest poetry is nothing compared to the fire in which it was produced. Milton testified to the appearance of *Paradise Lost* as a kind of dictation from the ether. He had no conscious control over the poem. At the end of this long meditation on what escapes, Shelley declares that poets are the 'hierophants of an unapprehended inspiration',[25] their legislation has the same relationship to the unapprehended as does their poetry.

Where does this argument lead? Suffice it to say that it is some distance from the positions of White or Weinrib. It is necessary to proceed poetically, to see how these themes are developed. *Ozymandias* is a poem about the law that can be read in the shadow of *A Defence of Poetry*:

> I met a traveller from an antique land
> Who said: 'Two vast and trunkless legs of stone
> Stand in the desert. Near them, on the sand,
> Half sunk, a shattered visage lies, whose frown,
> And wrinkled lip, and sneer of cold command,
> Tell that its sculptor well those passions read
> Which yet survive, stamped on those lifeless things,
> The hand that mocked them and the heart that fed;

---

[25] Shelley P.B., 'A Defence of Poetry' in Shawcross, J. (ed.), *Shelley's Literary and Philosophical Criticism* (London, Henry Frowde, 1909), 160.

And on the pedestal these words appear:
'My name is Ozymandias, king of Kings:
Look on my works, ye Mighty, and despair!'
Nothing beside remains. Round the decay
Of that colossal wreck, boundless and bare
The lone and level sands stretch far away.[26]

Ozymandias is a field alive with energies and counter-energies. There is a formal precision to its organisation, a sonnet consisting of four quatrains and a concluding couplet. One could discuss its rhyme scheme, its rhythm, movement and evocation of mood. One might read it as White recommends. *Ozymandias* provides a metaphor for a particular manifestation of tyrannical power that is self-justifying. However, reading the poem enacts a different process where readers must articulate their claims and dispute whose is the most compelling. Only in this way can claims to authority be justified. Unjustified claims, like the image of Ozymandias, are doomed to collapse. But this might not be satisfying. The poem does not conclude with an ethical message as such. Rather, like a *Dust of Snow*, it chooses not to reveal something in its strange concluding image.

To approach the representation of the law in this poem it is necessary to trace a peculiar set of concerns. The poem must be read as describing a more fundamental opposition between law and poetry. Ozymandias represents the law. It is necessary to stress first of all that Ozymandias is not a representation of any particular, modern form of law. The poem describes a kind of historical foundation for the very form of law, a source of possibility.[27] Ozymandias is taken to be a representation of Ramases II. Indeed, Ozymandias is the Greek name by which Ramases II was known. It carries associations of the way in which power clothes itself, dresses itself up and becomes spectacular. At a metaphoric level, this corresponds with a wider theme of revelation and occultation

---

[26] Shelley, P.B., *Selected Poems*, ed. Webb, T. (London, Everyman, 1977), 11.

[27] In Ch. 2, the image and modern law will be more thoroughly investigated.

that will be elaborated. Note, first of all, that Ramases II was the pharaoh in the time of Moses.

The law of Ramases is represented by the figure of the statue. The core of the poem, the ruination of the image of the emperor, could be read as informed by a broader Judaeo-Christian idea of the fall of false idols. This in turn states a counter-law, a law of divine inspiration and revelation: a true law of the spirit that opposes the secular, pagan law of the worldly power. Ozymandias' claim is one of profound hubris. His claims to empire come to nothing beside those of the laws of the true faith. These themes need to be elaborated. In the wider litera-ture on the roots of the law, there is this same concern with the image of law and the prohibition of counter, or non-licensed representations. Behind the classical fear of the image is a pecu-liar complex. Consider the Greek roots of the western tradi-tion.[28] At this point of origin there is a banishment of the image from the realm of the law and rational government. Shelley could have read this in Plato's *The Republic*, where the presence of poets and artists is inimical to the order of the common-wealth. Their evocations of utopias challenge the good order of the laws by making men unhappy with their lot. In *The Laws*, poetic discourse is defined as inherently ambiguous as it is impossible to find a clear statement of the truth in dramatic speeches that provide contrasting attitudes rather than the cer-tainties that the legislator requires. The poet or the artist, then, appears to challenge the philosopher's claims to order both the

[28] See Douzinas, C., 'Prosopon and Antiprosopon: Prolegomena for a Legal Iconology' in Douzinas, C., and Nead, L., *Law and the Image* (London, Routledge, 1999). The author shows that both the classical and the Judaeo-Christian traditions had a similar distrust of the image. For the Judaic tradition, the prohibition against images is fundamental, appearing as the second com-mandment, interpreted as banning Man 'from making graven images, or any likeness of anything that is in heaven above, or that is in earth beneath, or that in the water under the earth'. Within the rabbinic and scholarly traditions, such images were prohibited as they tended to distract from God's manifestation in the law, his presence in the word. The divine cannot be represented anthropo-morhically, as this would be to return to the body and the human, the world of fallen matter.

community and its discourse. Law has to be sovereign; it cannot countenance any source of legality other than itself. [29] But this is only a partial truth. The poem shows that this claim to sovereignty, either secular or spiritual, rings hollow.

How does this feed into a reading of this poem? Like the law, the poem reveals the same iconophobia. It shows the ruination of the law that relies on the image, and endeavours to put in its place . . . what? Something else? Poetry? Divine inspiration? The name of Shelley?

The power of the law is not just the power of the image, but the power to sustain its own name, a logic of memory that can be referred back to the image. Indeed, in this poem, the name and the image are inseparable. Ozymandias creates his power by naming himself and representing himself as the king of Kings.[30] The poem effectively plays off the name of the king and the name of the poet who has chosen to represent the king in ruins. *Ozymandias* is an indirect representation of the king; the poem is more properly the memorial of Shelley, who has caused Ozymandias to be remembered. It is perhaps in this

[29] See *ibid.*, 44–8. Douzinas goes on to argue that although the image is false, there is at the same time an acknowledgement of its necessity as a way of figuring the source of the law. Thus, it would be false to argue that the Christian tradition completely rejected the icon. It was more a case of distinguishing between good and bad images. The law had to rely on the image. The Byzantines allowed representations of the Eucharist and the cross. Likewise, Western Catholicism has a strong tradition of representation. What lies behind this is a question not so much of the evil distractions of the image, but the correct way in which the invisible, the transcendent and the all-powerful, the foundation of the law, should be manifested. Behind the image lies a contradictory desire both to 'stage and hide' (at 46) divinity. Although there is clearly a difference between the idea of God and the idea of the emperor as the source of law, in each discourse the image works with a similar logic. It embodies the absent source and makes it present. On the image and birth of secular law, see Goodrich, P., *Oedipus Lex* (Berkeley, Cal., University of California Press, 1995), 41–63, 68–71 and 108–38. Goodrich is concerned with the antirrhetic, the discourse against images in common law jurisprudence.

[30] In a similar way, law's name can be understood as a personification that suggests that law has an identity, and an ability to declare its own constitution. For law to survive as law, it has to remember, and cause others to remember, its name.

sense that the poet could be said to 'legislate', to mandate a memory through a successful creative act that rivals that of the sovereign. In this poem, the reader is left with the name of Shelley that records itself, for as long as this poem is read Shelley memorialises himself representing the fall of Ozymandias.

So, does Shelley's name represent the coming of another law that is linked to poetry? *Ozymandias* is a poem about the possibilities of poetry. The opening image represents the poem as a continuation of a traveller's tale, it forefronts the scene of telling and retelling, the act of remembering and transmitting a truth. Moreover, when the statue is described, the poem recalls the work of the mason who had created the representation; again, an act of creation that the poem continues. It could be said that *Ozymandias* foregrounds the scene of its own creation precisely to show that it has an origin. Ozymandias' claim to an originless and supreme power is mocked by this ability of the poem to capture and turn against it the power that the law has to claim for itself. Shelley's poetry is, then, a return to origin as a means of showing how the present is produced.

How is the ambiguous concluding image of the poem to be understood?

The sands stretching away into infinity may be a figure of time that will sweep away the poem, Ozymandias the King and the law. Alternatively, the desert may represent the space out of which the traveller comes with strange tales. It might also be suggested that, just as the law cannot be represented, the poem itself moves towards its own disappearance. When Shelley compared poets with legislators, he was trying to conjure this strange energy. Poetry summons 'something' that is excessive, that exceeds form and content. Notes on the composition of Shelley's poetry by Mary Shelley assist in tracing the flight of what escapes the poem. She writes that thoughts would come to Shelley, find a momentary form, and then vanish into silence again. Inspiration was a mocking 'wild spirit'.[31] The poet frequently fell

[31] Mary Shelley's notes on the poems of 1817 in *The Poetical Works of Shelley* (Oxford, Oxford University Press, 1952), 551.

into despair with his writing for this reason. A completed poem was a failure; what had made for its composition might never return. Interestingly, at this time Shelley was working on a translation of a Homeric hymn to Mercury. Mercury was the god of messages between gods and mortals. One possible figure for the unpredictable wild spirit that kindled Shelley's verse is indeed this avatar.

Ozymandias shares with the law the power to mandate form, to create foundations, to give form to the spirit of what may come to be.

Conclusion: up against it

At the time of writing of the poem Shelley was engaged, at both a personal and political level, in opposition to the law. A bitter custody case over the children from his first marriage, presided over by Lord Eldon, was taking place against the background of popular political agitation for universal suffrage.[32] The government was responding with repressive measures.[33] Shelley composed a pamphlet[34] and organised meetings. Risking the obvious, it might be suggested that *Ozymandias* represents Shelley's aesthetic response. Law is inflexible, undemocratic, concerned only with the preservation of an old order. Like Ozymandias, it is bound to crumble to nothing. Shelley's stance

[32] Holmes, R., *Shelley The Pursuit* (London, Penguin, 1974), 356–7, 410–11. The case began on 24 January 1817. Judgment against the poet was given in March of the next year. *Ozymandias* was probably begun in December 1817, and published in January 1818. Mary Shelley, *ibid.*, 551, writes '[n]o words can express the anguish he felt when his elder children were torn from him . . . [a]t one time, while the question was still pending, the Chancellor had said some words that seemed to intimate that Shelley should not be permitted the care of any of his children . . .'. It would thus not be entirely unreasonable to suggest that the composition of *Ozymandias* reflects a time when Shelley found himself up against the law. In a letter to Byron in January 1818, the courts are described as 'tribunals of tyranny and superstition'.
[33] In March 1818, Habeas Corpus was suspended and The Seditious Meetings Act was passed.
[34] 'A Proposal for Putting Reform to the vote throughout the Kingdom'.

as a rebel against the law makes it is necessary for him to spec-
ify what will replace the law. The traditional aesthetic response
would be to retire inwards, opposing a noble soul to brute reality. *Ozymandias* suggests, however, that Shelley's own name, the
promise of the poetry that he will write, his own imagination of
utopia, provides an energy that could summon other laws, other
ideas of community.

This chapter has argued that an aesthetics of law has not
taken the path suggested by Shelley's work. It has limited itself
either to a rigid formalism, or an insistence that the law can learn
from an ethics of literary language. *Ozymandias* shows that the
aesthetic offers a challenge to the order of the law, a promise of
a different law.

However, the question still remains; to what extent is law an
aesthetic phenomenon? The next chapter will pick up another
insight of Shelley's poem. Law's hold over the social world can
be compared to the fascinating hold of the image over the spec-
tator. To elaborate this claim, it is necessary to turn to a more
self-consciously critical form of legal writing. Critical Legal
Studies takes seriously the idea that law is an image.[35]

[35] Apart from the attention given to the image in Critical Legal scholarship,
it also seems particularly suitable for a development of the present project as it
describes itself as an aesthetics, albeit in a 'fragmentary' sense. See Kennedy, D.,
'First Year Teaching as Political Action' (1980) *Journal of Law and Social
Problems* 47, 52.

[36] Critical is meant here in a non-Kantian or Marxist sense. Although these
two reference points do not define the field, they can offer some orientating
sense. Thus, a critical aesthetics of law is neither an attempt to posit a regula-
tory ideal for law, nor a privileged external site for critique. A critical aesthetics
could possibly be co-ordinated with Jacques Derrida's notion of deconstruction
as expressed in the 'The Force of Law: The "Mystical Foundation of
Authority"' in Cornell, D., Rosenfeld, M., and Gray Carlson, D. (eds.),
Deconstruction and the Possibility of Justice eds. (London, Routledge, 1992),
3–68. Deconstruction can be glossed as a 'maximum intensification of a transformation in progress' (9). It might be possible to understand this cryptic

Can Critical Legal Studies repeat Shelley's romantic gesture against the alienation of the law? Could there be a critical aesthetics of law?[36]

expression as a call to produce new readings of texts that are themselves in constant transformation as they are read, re-read and debated. It would also be to commit to a form of politics that, in Richard Beardsworth's words, is progressive as it seeks the invention of a 'democracy to come'. See *Derrida and the Political* (London, Routledge, 1996). As far as its intervention in the law school and legal pedagogy is concerned, this could be a bringing together of a 'deconstruction motivated by literary theory' or philosophy and 'critical legal studies' (at 9) to produce radical approaches to problems in jurisprudence focused on questions of legitimacy and authority. For an elaboration of this position, and what it could mean for a programme in law and literature, see Goodrich, P. 'Law by Other Means' (1998) 10 *Cardozo Studies in Law and Literature* 111–16 .

2
Lie Dream of a Legal Soul
Critical Legal Studies and the
Theory of the Image

To begin again: Critical Legal Studies (CLS) appropriated aesthetics to provide an understanding of the centrality of the image to legal language. This may appear unusual as the aesthetic is seen primarily as a theory of art, and legal language as a process of reasoning. However, if CLS is placed in its historical context, it is possible to understand how a progressive movement made use of what was at hand to further the urgent task of critique. Just as the image represents and distorts reality by making what is fluid appear fixed and unchanging, law is criticised as a reification of the world.[1] A construction of the social world is presented

---

[1] In this chapter the words 'alienation' and 'reification' will be used as suggesting aspects of the same process. The notion of alienation perhaps reaches its most important modern development in Marx's *Capital*, although it has important beginnings in Judaeo-Christian theology, Hegel's *Phenomenology of Mind* and Feurbach's critique of Hegel. In summary, alienation in *Capital* describes the conditions of social existence in capitalist society. Those who do not own the means of production become alienated from both the process of production and products, which appear to emanate from autonomous economic/industrial/commercial operations over which there is little or no control. Reification also suggests this sense in which things produced become independent of the process of production and appear to dominate the social world. As alienation and reification are also elements of a theory of consciousness, it could be said that they operate at an ideological level, i.e. at the level of beliefs, ideas, understandings and practices. CLS could be broadly conceived as attempting to theorise the law as alienation. Thus, the work of Gabel and Kennedy to be considered below takes as its starting point the notion that law is an ideological distortion of the world. Ideas/practices of law have to be examined to see how they interface with wider social, economic and political concerns. At the same time, any notion of alienation in their work also carries other philosophical echoes. It

25

as the only possible way of ordering communal life. Law makes use of the image to give a sense of its own continuity and centrality to social being. What are the consequences of this critique? Can law be unmasked to reveal the image? We will see that it is not a question of *simply* associating law and the image with ideology and distortion. The increasing adoption of psychoanalytic theory by scholars within a CLS 'tradition' intensifies this problematic. Psychoanalysis can provide insights into the image as the foundation of the law, but it also creates further problems. At worst it finds an inescapable law of the father inscribed in the human soul and makes any kind of resistance unthinkable. Alienation thus becomes constitutive of the subject, rather than a product of political processes that can be changed: we are trapped in the structures that define us. The risk is that a critical aesthetics disappears in its very moment of foundation. Unless psychoanalysis is used creatively to show that the structure of law is open to reinvention, aesthetics teaches us no more than a stoic acceptance of our troubled condition.

How to operate with a blown mind: law, the image and alienation

Perhaps the beginnings of Critical Legal Studies seem rather distant now. To gain a perspective one would have to turn back to the radicalism of the 1960s and 1970s. Bob Dylan's song *When the Ship Comes In* evokes the utopianism of those times:

> Then they'll raise their hands
> Sayin' we'll meet all your demands
> But we'll shout from the bows your days are numbered.
> And like Pharaoh's tribe,
> They'll be drowned in the tide,
> And like Goliath they'll be conquered.[2]

would not be sufficient simply to interpret CLS as suggesting that alienation is limited to capitalist social relations. For an introduction to CLS, see Kelman, M., *A Guide to Critical Legal Studies* (Cambridge, Mass., Harvard University Press, 1987) 1–15.

[2] Dylan, B., *Lyrics 1962–1985* (London, Jonathan Cape, 1987), 101.

Ozymandias appears again, this time swept away by the tide of the Red Sea that brings the revolution and the overthrow of social and political idols. Although Dylan's song reflects a slightly earlier moment of the civil liberties struggle, it suggests the ferment from which CLS emerged, a revolt against the generals and the grey men who were responsible for Vietnam. The world was being destroyed in the name of secure markets for capitalism.[3] In these times it was difficult to retain faith in the neutrality of the law. Critical Legal Studies can be aligned with the contemporary counter culture that was attempting to articulate a total critique of social and political relationships. For want of a better description, it can be perceived as a romantic movement that opposed life to law.

Life could be linked with any number of values, but it was essentially the space of self-creation linked to the insistence that the world could be different. Some visions of the good society contained ideas of law transformed, others did not.[4] CLS was concerned with those moments when life reasserted itself in spontaneous actions or counter-cultural activities. In one notorious example, it was the time before the teacher came into class; in another, the moment of authentic exchange between bank clerks when management was not looking. It might also be what happened when you were smoking a doobie or the famous 'intersubjective zap'.[5] Clearly, life exists not as a thought-out political doctrine, but as a provocation, a utopian urge for a better world.

These notions inform the tensions that animate the 'fundamental contradiction'. In its most pithy formulation, the contradiction expresses the troubled nature of social life: 'relations with

[3] See Schlag, P., 'U.S. CLS' [1999] *Law and Critique* 199–210.

[4] See Gabel, P., 'Ontological Passivity and the Constitution of Otherness within Large Scale Social Networks' cited in Kennedy, D., and Gabel, P., 'Roll Over Beethoven' (1984) *Stanford Law Review* 24–5. 'Intersubjective zap' is also drawn from this piece. It is defined as: 'a sudden, intuitive moment of connectedness. It is a vitalizing moment of energy [hence "zap"] when the barriers between the self and the other are in some way suddenly dissolved'.

[5] 'Roll Over Beethoven', n. 4 *supra*, 32.

others are both necessary and incompatible with our freedom'.[6] The contradiction is an insight into both the problems of the existing order and the limitations of collective action in the name of a new society. As it is 'fundamental' the contradiction means that any attempt to achieve an 'unalienated collective existence'[7] through social action risks reducing the individual to the coercive demands of the group, and thus duplicating the problem that social action had tried to resolve. Despite the disavowal of this notion by the 'crits' themselves,[8] it is still worthy of attention. For a start, it absolves CLS of believing in a simple notion of a pure, revolutionary social being. Indeed, 'the very structures against which we rebel are necessarily within us as well as outside us. We are implicated in what we would transform, and it in us'.[9] The fundamental contradiction describes a strange politics. It is still necessary to think and act, to affirm a transformative political programme, but we must proceed with 'faith and hope' rather than any 'assurance of reason'.[10] Is it possible to act without reason? How are 'faith and hope' to be conceived within this process? A notion of teleology, of assured outcomes, must be distinguished from the sense in which actions and decisions are made and justified. The former has to be rejected, whilst the latter is somehow preserved. Untangling these meanings raises complex questions, not least those theological echoes that can be heard in 'faith and hope'. For the moment, these will have to be left to resonate and await a more thorough investigation. More pressing is the need to explicate the links between the contradiction and psychoanalytic discourse. It will be argued that the positing of alienation as the basis of social being makes psychoanalytic theory particularly suitable to carry forward the legacy of CLS. There is another connection. Within psychoanalysis, there is the same balancing of hope and despair. Whilst

---

[6] Kennedy, D., 'The Structure of Blackstone's Commentaries' in (1979) 28 *The Buffalo Law Review* 7.

[7] *Ibid.*, 6.

[8] For a criticism of the term, see Kennedy and Gabel, n. 5 *supra*, 16–26.

[9] Kennedy, n. 6 *supra*, 6.

[10] *Ibid.*, 7.

knowing that social being is inherently traumatic, this must not become the occasion for despair. The task is to see how psychoanalysis can move law in a progressive direction.

The fundamental contradiction is thus founded on a notion of constitutive alienation. To some extent, a failure to investigate the dynamics of this process did perhaps account for its untimely fall from favour. For the idea to become live again, it is necessary to show that a theory of alienation understands the image as central to the production of subjectivity at both an individual and communal level.[11] Legal theory must take seriously the reliance of the law on the image. Consider the panoply of images that characterise legal practice from the architecture of the courtroom to the formalities of legal dress and behaviour. These images serve to impress upon the viewer the majesty of the law, demonstrating law's history, autonomy and continuity. But the theory goes further than merely noting architecture or tradition. A more radical claim is being made.[12] The legitimacy of the social world is

[11] The aesthetic can be thought of as essential to a materialist philosophy. The very term aesthetics can itself be derived from the Greek *aisthesis;* the realm of the human perception, of sensation in the material, see Eagleton, T., *The Ideology of the Aesthetic* (Oxford, Blackwell, 1990), 13. 'Aesthetic is the whole of our sensate life together—the business of affections and aversions, of how the world strikes the body on its sensory surfaces, of that which takes root in the gaze and the guts and all that arises from our most banal, biological insertion into the world'. Aesthetics is thus a way of understanding the human subject as fallen or as inserted into a sensuous world. This subject is the somatic subject; the subject of passions and emotions. In short the embodied subject. It is precisely this fleshy subject that CLS has tried to describe; and it is attempting this description that is CLS' most radical gesture. It is opposed to the subject of liberal legal thought, which most often appears as an abstraction, removed from any bodily life, unsexed and of no race. This approach would have certain correspondences with aspects of Manderson's important vision of an aesthetic jurisprudence in Manderson , D., 'Beyond the Provincial: Spaces, Aesthetics and Modernist Legal Theory' [1996] *Melbourne Law Review* 1048. The vision of an aesthetics of uncertainty and surprise could certainly be co-ordinated with the material as read through Shelley in Ch. 6 of the present work. The distinction between an aesthetics of geometry, as expressed by formalism, and geography, as expressed by pluralism, would also elaborate the distinction between Weinrib and White in Ch. 1.

[12] For a theoretically informed analysis of legal architecture, see Haldar, P. 'Acoustic Justice' in Bentley, L., and Flynn, L. (eds.), *Law and the Senses:*

sustained by 'overpowering' symbols that extend over the whole operation of the law.[13] Viewed from the perspective of today, where the proliferation of advertising and branding[14] is extensive, it may appear that the regime of the image is a feature of the post-modern condition, rather than fundamental to the discourse of law. However, it would be possible to trace the condition back to the very constitution of social being in religions and mythologies that united the faithful around images of their deities. This begin-ning is also where the roots of Roman law or common law could be located. Thus, as far as the image is concerned, the difference between the ancient and the post-modern is a matter of degree. The very constitution of both ancient and modern society rests on the communal acceptance of an image that represents the founder, whether God, King, law, nation or constitution. This brief description, no doubt, begs many questions. Tracing the

Sensational Jurisprudence (London, Pluto Press, 1996) 123–36. See also 'The Function of Ornament in Quintillian, Alberti and Court Architecture' in Douzinas, C., and Nead, L., *Law and the Image* (Chicago, Ill., University of Chicago Press, 1999). For a consideration of historical aspects of the common law tradition, see Raffield, P., 'The Separate Art Worlds of Dreamland and Drunkeness: Elizabethan Revels at the Inns of Court' in *Law and Critique* Vol VIII, no 2 (1997) 163–88.

[13] One of the key early texts is Bankowski, Z., and Maugham, G., *Images of Law* (London, Routledge, 1976). Behind the image of law is the nakedness of class power. Law as image is synonymous with false consciousness. Capitalist law, even in its liberal manifestations, can be though of as obfuscation; a confi-dence trick that hides the true, exploitative reality: 'We call this book images of law because we counterpoint the images of freedom that the law raises with their reality, enslavement'. (xii). A revolutionary Marxism that sees an outside to power and conceives of a utopia where law has 'withered away' fuels Bankowski and Maugham's passion. For a more sophisticated elaboration, see Kennedy, D., 'The Role of Law in Economic Thought: Essays on the Fetishism of Commodities' (1985), 34 *The American University Law Review* 939–1001.

[14] See Debord, G., *The Society of the Spectacle* (Detriot, Black and Red, 1983) and one of its more recent rewritings, Klein, N., *No Logo* (London, Flamingo, 2000). For an introduction to the legal spectacle see Goodrich, P., *Languages of Law* (London, Weidenfeld and Nicolson, 1990), 297–319. Any thinking through of a legal situationalism would have to take account of McDonald, A., 'The New Beauty of a Sum of Possibilites' (1997) 8 *Law and Critique*. 141–59 and Stanley, C., *Urban Excess and the Law* (London, Cavendish, 1996).

precise modifications of the regime of images remains a task outside the realms of this book, but it seems both theoretically defensible and experientially resonant that social and political order is legitimised and perpetuated by images. The pressing task is to isolate the legal spectacle.

Law may communicate in the logic of legal arguments, but it is also reliant on the image. Images are as much part of law's institutionalisation as the more obvious manifestations of its power in the courts, the police force and authoritative texts. There are at least two related aspects to the notion of the law as image. First, if law is described as an ensemble of images, then more broadly this becomes a description of law's misrepresentation of the world. The Image is associated with a process that rigidifies and abstracts from a fluid social reality.[15] Consider legal reasoning. It subsumes diverse, individual situations under general, abstract rules. This process presupposes certain cultural assumptions that allow situations to be appreciated as similar or dissimilar in the first place. These contingent relations are then effectively seen as examples of the rule, their dissimilarity neutralised. The world becomes 'frozen' in its existing realities.[16] These realities are then appreciated as an adequate representation of what the world *is*. Insight is achieved when suddenly one sees through this process. The law effectively denies that the world could be otherwise, but precisely because the world is constructed, it can be made again through conscious activity. Everyday disgruntlement could lead to an 'explosion', a realisation that breaks through the normally passive acceptance of the system and its functioning: 'fuck this bullshit'.[17]

---

[15] Gabel, P., 'Reification in Legal Reasoning' (1980) 3 *Research in Law and Sociology* 34. See also Kennedy, D., 'Form and Substance in Private Law Adjudication' (1976) *Harvard Law Review* 1685 and Gabel, P., 'The Phenomenology of Rights–Consciousness and the Pact of the Withdrawn Selves' (1984) 62 *Texas Law Review* 1563–99.

[16] Gabel, P., 'Reification in Legal Reasoning', n. 15 *supra*, 27.

[17] *Ibid.*, 34. Also see the film *Falling Down* (Warner 1992, Kopelson, A., Herschel, W., Harris, T.,) for a contemporary and problematic study of social alienation.

Law is a kind of confidence trick, a way of making society appear. If one is not aware that legal concepts are reified and abstracted, they appear to have some kind of foundational substance, a kind of autonomy or independent being. This loses sight of the notion that the system manufactures its own conditions of legitimacy and then attempts to legislate them as *a priori* universals that have a legitimising effect through their appeal to reason. To borrow a Marxist term, this process of reification is a corruption of the very process of reasoning: it passes off one thing as another and gives a coherence and a substance to things that can have no independent being.

Although this argument may be persuasive, the persistence of law would still have to be explained. If the law was merely an elaborate trick, it would collapse if its subjects simply stopped believing. There must, in other words, be more to law's hold over the social world, and hence another aspect to the operation of the image. CLS argued that people continue to think and act within reified social relationships because reification conceals a deeper void. This absence of connectedness is so profound that it is traumatic. Cohesion of the social is provided through law's image of a united and regulated society. One imagines that social experience is one of 'harmonious co-existence'[18] under the protection of the law. Law gives a comforting sense of community. Indeed, in a time when other socially powerful ideas of community appear to be in crisis, law appears to be the last great ideal that can be articulated and defended. Law's images operate as a 'psychic gratification', holding back a deeper and more terrifying absence. To refer back to the previous arguments, this is an inauthentic notion of community. Law's sense of community is already reified, an element of false consciousness. Group feeling re-presented through legal categories is disconnected from any more fundamental emotional grounding.

Is this argument convincing? The key problem with CLS, or the 'question that killed critical legal studies'[19] is the issue of what

[18] Gabel, 'Reification in Legal Reasoning', n 15 *supra*.

[19] Fischl, R. M., 'The Question that Killed Critical Legal Studies' (1992) 17 *Law and Social Inquiry* 779–829.

would replace the law. If contemporary society is alienated and rotten, how should we continue? Could the law be swept away? To see CLS in such a way would certainly be to identify certain revolutionary aspects in its makeup. Within this paradigm, the question of the role of law after the revolution is somewhat vague. Even if the re-definitions of socialist legality in communist states are not taken as a guide to post revolutionary 'law', CLS appears to amount to no more than utopian hopes that the world could be made a better place. However, such a way of reading arguably obscures the true potential of critical thinking, and limits it to an unnecessarily restricted idea of Marxism. It is also a misreading of CLS to the extent that it suggests that a society can do without its foundational images, its controlling fictions. It can never be a simple question of replacing 'capitalist law' with 'post-capitalist' law. As has been pointed out, it is not useful to talk as if law had a 'place' and CLS offered a set of tools to redefine this place: 'the *point* of critical legal scholarship is that the law is far better understood as a significant aspect of the complex interplay between our culture and our structures of thought'.[20] Refusing to see CLS as merely a revolutionary movement directs attention to difficult questions about our constitution as social beings. CLS should be perceived as pioneering the study of what increasingly constitutes and dominates the social: the regime of the image. But can the theory of alienation and reification provide insights in the way that it is deployed by CLS scholars?[21]

In providing such a wide-ranging account of alienation, CLS could be accused of effectively destroying the creativity it was attempting to discover. If the world were reified to the extent

[20] *Ibid.*, 802.

[21] Gabel, 'Reification in Legal Reasoning', n. 15 *supra*, 36. Reification is not just an account of the construction of a reality by political processes. It appears that it describes something more 'fundamental' to our experience of the world. Reification can also describe a process that goes on in everyday language, if the concept is understood as a use of language that 'seizes'. It could be represented as a process that is secondary to our primary experience of the world which is temporal: the world is experienced as an ongoing set of situations and events.

described, where could uncontaminated ideas be found? The radical attempt to reveal the possibilities of the social world finds nothing but the triumph of the law. However, this would again be a misreading of the possibilities that CLS offered. CLS glimpsed the notion that although images are essential to the production of the social, images can be contested.[22] This problematic was increasingly articulated in psychoanalytical terms, and this turn now needs to be examined. Psychoanalysis must be read as an attempt to define the existence of social being as alienated consciousness, and to see this as the condition of contemporary social and legal thought. Dissident appropriations of the thought of the French analyst Jacques Lacan offer the most promising radical understandings of the aesthetic dimensions of the legal fantasm.

The abortionist's relation to limbo: psychoanalysis and alienation

Psychoanalysis appeared useful to CLS as it provided one of the most thoroughly worked out perspectives on alienation. In a Lacanian understanding, alienation cannot be avoided. This takes the CLS insight into the nature of the reificatory qualities of language a step further to become a more thorough account of subjectivity resting upon alienation in language. It might be easy to argue that such a theory is inherently reactionary and productive of political quietism. However, this position is a useful starting point for an aesthetics of law. Psychoanalysis can account for both the roots of institutional law and the instability of this foundation. This last point is fundamental. Law, read through psychoanalysis, is not reduced to an essential, a historical set of foundations, resistant to change. Psychoanalysis makes possible a critique of law.

---

[22] This is explored in a reference to image in the legal order of feudalism. The images that were relied upon to support the feudal order were simultaneously an expression of 'love . . . and possible salvation'. Although these images operate to give people a promise of community, they do so in a way that ultimately supports their alienation. They derive from 'the emotional correlate of reification'. *Ibid.*, 45.

Lawyers have approached psychoanalysis as offering potential insights into the nature of the law as a kind of language. Lacan himself comments that:

> To . . . a jurist who had been kind enough to inquire about my discourse, I felt I could respond—in order to give him a sense of its foundation, namely that language is not the speaking being.[23]

This enigmatic statement is explained somewhat by reference to the law school where the 'existence of codes makes it clear that language consists therein'. The usefulness of psychoanalysis to law is that the former helps define the constitution of the latter in terms of 'codes' of language that define those who speak them. This may appear hopelessly confusing. One would imagine that language is defined and spoken by people, rather than the other way round. To clarify this insight, we must follow psychoanalysis' tracking of the origins of law to the 'human condition', a study of the drama of the individual subject's birth into desire and language.

Lacan has commented that it is interesting that so many words that describe the act of 'putting into the world' are at root 'juridicial'.[24] The psychoanalytic theory of desire is no exception. It makes use of Freud's own interpretation of the object of desire, *das Ding*. The French translation of Freud's German goes back to the Latin *causa*, a word that is connected with the law, indicating a hearing, or a proceeding.[25] How can this be developed? One can speak of the enjoyment of a legal right. This might suggest that there is some link between pleasure and law. Law carefully controls how a legal right can be enjoyed. But where does enjoyment take us? Psychoanalysis would seek to define a primal law that relates to desire and pleasure. The following description will attempt to approach this law.

As the child is brought into the world by the desire of its parents it could be said that the 'subject is caused by the desire

[23] Lacan, J., *Seminar XX* (New York, Norton, 1998) 2.
[24] *Ibid.*, 214.
[25] *Ibid.*, 43.

of the other'.[26] Desiring to be desired, the child will come to consciousness needing to rely on an other that is beyond them, with whom they can never completely identify. Once within the world, the subject becomes aware both of being an object of desire and of him or herself having desires that always recur and cannot be satisfied. Acquiring language, the child will have to learn to express the desire for something that they cannot have: a complete identification with the mother. This trauma accounts for the unconscious. At the moment when one enters language, the moment when one acquires subjectivity, the subject experiences a disjuncture, a gap where the unconscious could be 'located'. In this sentence 'locate' has to appear in quotation marks, as it is strictly impossible to speak of the unconscious. It is the 'unrealised'. To the extent that the unconscious shows itself, it is through dreams, slips of the tongue, obsessional behaviour or other pathologies that are symptoms of an attempt to articulate a reconnection with the 'real' that is inaccessible to the subject.

The famous statement that the unconscious is structured like a language is perhaps another way of looking into this place of shadows. The existence of the unconscious is not to be related to something hidden which comes to the surface, or some romantic source of creativity or pure instinctual life. On the contrary, it could be understood as what separates from instinctual life. It is the mark of a subject who lacks, who is divided from a source of being. The unconscious seems to exist on a plane with desire. Indeed the condition of desire is related to the existence of an unconscious, if this is to be taken as a structure which escapes the subject and that can be compared to language. When the child becomes a speaking/thinking subject in language, identification between it and the signifier is not possible, because the signifier receives its identity only in the series of signifiers that make up language, the system of differences. If desire is always desire for something else, something other, and the

---

[26] Fink, B., in Feldstein, R., Fink, B., Jaanus, M. (eds.), *Reading Seminar XI: Lacan's* 'Four Fundamental Concepts of Psychoanalysis' (Albany, NY, State University of New York Press, 1995), 78.

structure of the subject is such that it is always forced to desire, it is at home in language which permanently defers. At this stage another important notion needs to be introduced. Language exists before the subject. The child is born into a pre-existing world. Just as the contents of the world, objects and people, can appear meaningfully only in language, language is the place where subjects must deploy and locate their desire.

To elaborate this description, it is necessary to show that the image is central to the entrance into language. In psychoanalytic discourse, the image is the imago that allows the individual to establish a relationship between itself and its world. Born too soon, lacking motor co-ordination and the ability to care for itself, the human subject is immediately given over to the care of another. Trapped in an ill co-ordinated body, the child is drawn to the image as a representation of a coherent sense of self. Bear in mind, though, that this is 'an alienating identity'.[27] Identifying with the imago, the child recognises his/her reflection in the mirror. The mirror phase is thus predestined; human subjectivity presupposes the mirror stage. The formation of personality is a dialectical process as it propels the subject towards a more profound identification with language. A more complex sense of the self is made to correspond with the name and with personal and impersonal pronouns. To have a social identity, the individual has to become a being in and of language. One must master the basic separation which allows any human subject to enter into language and understand that becoming a mature speaker of words means accepting that to speak of yourself is to represent yourself, and thus, in a very real sense, to be absent from your words. Language employs signs or words that represent or replace absent 'things'. The separation of the self from the self, which allows the self to become an object to the self, is the basic and fundamental structure of subjectivity. It has to include the loss of something that might always be nothing (what one was before one could speak). To have a constitutive image, to accede to speech, is thus to lose any sense of real unity. At the same

---

[27] Lacan J., *Ecrits* (London, Tavistock, 1977), 4.

time there is a desire for unity and for a sense of being a complete self. This desire is the key for understanding the subject who has to interpret his own image in the torment of separation.

If this can be imagined as a process, it is completed when the father interposes himself between the child and the other's desire. Already biologically separated from the mother, the separation of the child's desire for the mother is completed by the name of the father. In this drama of the subject, the symbolic support of the law appears. It is necessary to follow through the idea on two levels: what the name of the father means for the subject of desire, and how this translates into a broader sense of law and desire. Traced above is the trauma of the subject's entrance into language. This has to involve a separation from the unity with the maternal figure. Be careful here. There is certainly a tendency within this kind of thought to fetishise contingent social and gender relationships. This makes for numerous problems that cannot be properly addressed in this book. The fundamental point seems to be that the child has a relationship with a primary carer, and this relationship must always be interrupted by another. Once the relationship is interrupted, the name of the father comes to signify for the child the desire of the mother, ultimately, the desire of the Other (in that the Other will be created as the order into which the child must locate herself; the desire for the mother becomes associated with the world and what it wants of the individual). Again, perhaps the language is deceptive. The name of the father is an algebraic symbol, an empty space that could be replaced with any signifier designating what takes the mother's desire from the child. Once the child can understand, at the level of language, the substitution of the name of the father for the desire of the mother, the child has begun to understand the substitutions of signification. But there is still something mysterious and inexpressible in the other's desire, a missing factor: *objet petit a. Objet petit a* is unidentifiable, it can only be guessed. It could be the remains of what always satisfied desire, the original unity. As a reminder of what cannot be remembered, it is an object destined to reappear in fantasies and dreams as the object of desire. How might this make for a broader structure of law?

Desire can provide both the foundation for the law and, also, in that there is always something that escapes, that continues to provoke desire, something that might suggest that the law's foundation is never firm.

Lacanian psychoanalysis finds the primordial law in the imposition of culture on nature in the form of the incest taboo that treats the mother and the sister as forbidden objects. The name of the father and the structure of kinship come together to create the prohibition that allows genealogy and lineage. However, it would seem that the law, rather than simply being a prohibition, rests on forbidding what it creates. The name of the father in this sense is an enabler of desire: '. . . [t]he desire for the mother cannot be satisfied because it is the end, the terminal point, the abolition of the whole world of demand, which is at the deepest structural levels of man's unconscious'. In more explicitly Freudian terms, this could be theorised as the emergence of the super ego. The 'super ego' is based on the command 'enjoy', it is a 'correlate of castration'.[28] The law creates the desire for what it prohibits. Consider the Ten Commandments. These can be read as a kind of basic statement of what it means to speak. The incest prohibition is missing from the list of commandments. Speech is predicated on what cannot appear to it: forbidden enjoyment.

When Lacan talks of desire, he introduces the term *jouissance*. *Jouissance* might be described as the enjoyment of desire. To enter language, one has to renounce a certain *jouissance*. So much would follow from the idea of castration outlined above. As *jouissance* passes through the other, but cannot be satisfied by the other, it could be figured as prompting a demand that haunts the subject: '*Che voui?*' What do you want? The other is itself 'barred' because it is itself the realm of the expression of language, and desire that forever defer their objects. *Jouissance* could thus also be related to the fantasy that makes both the other and subject whole:

> Fantasy appears . . . as an answer to Che voui? to the unbearable enigma of the desire of the other, of the lack in the other; but it is at

[28] Lacan, n. 27 *supra*, 7.

the same time fantasy which . . . provides the coordinates of our desire—which constructs the frame enabling us to desire something.[29]

Fantasy is not a distraction from the constitution of the subject; it is the very source of identity. It might be suggested that the experience of love is fundamentally the experience of the fantasm. Kristeva has written that there is always something in love that tends towards power and sovereignty. Perhaps it is not surprising, then, to find that the structure of *jouissance* also makes for a structure of law.[30] To build the description, the law figures as one answer to the question *Che Voui?* The key question for the institution of the law is how to make itself constitute a symbolic order that will sustain the subject. It is necessary that the symbolic order be organised and articulated in such a way that the subject can find itself reflected in social institutions and thus gain a viable sense of social being. From this perspective an entire jurisprudence that describes the necessity of law for civilised being can be read not so much as a historical truth, nor as an ideological distortion, but as one possible fate for the social conditions of subjectivity.

Working within this tradition, the French historian and analyst Pierre Legendre has written: 'the term enjoyment, if one gives it the meaning which psychoanalysis borrowed from Law, simply refers to the inscription of the human body in the mythological order of an unconscious fantasm'.[31] The fantasm has to capture and regulate the desires of the group. At the most basic level, this would be to determine kinship patterns, the legitimacy of marriage and personal relationships. More sophisticated patterns of law determine what rights over property can be *enjoyed*. The law determines what can be owned, and how it can be owned. It regulates what can be inherited, what counts as public and private.

[29] Lacan, n. 27 *supra*, 313.

[30] Kristeva, J., *Tales of Love* (New York, Columbia University Press, 1987), 125.

[31] Goodrich, P. (ed.), *Law and the Unconscious, A Legendre Reader* (London, Macmillan, 1999), 129.

Legendre considers law's articulation of social foundations as essential to all social order. This broader understanding is termed dogmatic communication. Dogmatic communication is the transmission of the fundamental social myth. The 'structure' of this knot that ties the subject to the institution can be divined by reference to St. Augustine. St. Augustine described the 'liturgical order' as a 'structure of love'. Although referring to the Church, Legendre interprets Augustine as expressing a general truth: the subject must fall in love with the institution. Privileged in this attaching of the subject to the institution is the discourse of Roman law. Roman law is a discourse that allows the truth to appear,[32] it lays down a way of 'staging' functions which psychoanalysis considers necessary to social being, the institution and reproduction of human life. This is a 'non-negotiable principle'[33] or a 'principle of universal legislation'.[34] Identifying this principle means stripping away discourses on popular rights that have proved obstructive of the truth of Roman law. Roman law has shown itself to be flexible, adapting itself to various historical contexts, from its formal use in the development of the common law tradition to the more concrete way in which it provided the axioms for the law of the Holy See. Even when Roman law is most forgotten, or when, as at present, 'science' attempts to usurp its prerogatives, its essential function cannot be replaced or ignored.[35]

Must it be the fate of humanity to become subject of the institution, to love no more than the law? Whilst desire gives the law its hold over the individual and the social world, desire always goes beyond any particular institutional manifestation. It cannot be a question of turning to an outside of the law, as one is always

[32] Legendre, P., L'Empire de la Vérité: *Introduction aux espaces dogmatiques industriels* (Paris, Fayard, 1983), 132.

[33] Goodrich, n. 31 *supra*, 116.

[34] *Ibid.*, 116.

[35] That function is the 'mythological' foundation of the social bond; and it can be demonstrated by reference to the scholasticism of the Middle Ages that concerned the reception of Gratian's Decretals in around 1140 and the composition of the first glosses and commentaries in the mid 1300s. Scholasticism develops the materials that allows law to speak. *Ibid.*, 121.

within desire. The question could be rephrased as how, or where, one might find the potential of redefining the law, of making the law different. What would it mean to desire a different law? This could be thought of as a reopening of the question that was posed by CLS: where are the resources that can oppose a form of association and solidarity to that mandated by the law?

Castration and critique

There are no easy answers. One has to conceive of the possibility of critique within psychoanalysis, rather than seeing psychoanalysis as invalidating any form of critique. It is necessary to go back to the fundamental idea of psychoanalysis. To enter the social world is to be castrated. This is, of course, an idea that operates at a symbolic level. It refers to a founding metaphor that can take any number of specific forms. It can be understood as suggesting that prior to human subjects is a function that produces them, a wound that goes before them and makes them what they are. It accords to a fundamental sense of the loss, the void, finitude, limitedness or tragedy that lies behind what we do, and has always informed the great religious, aesthetic and legal structures that have defined culture and provided rituals and supports to sustain life. To criticise this particular vision of the social is to try and fashion a critical discourse. It would, of course, be suspicious and particularly reductive if psychoanalysis was no more than an apologetics for existing institutions. There has to be a way of thinking a fluid relationship between institutions and those whom they claim to speak for or represent.

To start again: the legal fantasm mandates ideas of title, right and inheritance as structures into which one fits. It defines social life in essentially legal terms, effectively providing a grid that articulates relationships between people. Jurisprudentially it has always been argued that the law puts an end to the war of all against all. Against this vision was opposed an inherent sociality that was ruined by law. There is no real point in continuing the argument about whether or not 'mankind' is by nature good or evil. A critique of law can start from a different point. There is a way in which human relationships can be imagined as within law, but constantly challenging the forms of the law that chose to represent those relationships. There is a 'gap' between the form of law at any one time and its possible reinvention, a different fantasm. This follows from the logic of castration and the structure of *jouissance*.

Consider the function of the phallus. Above it was argued that it is the possibility of signification emerging in the first place. When Lacan considers the phallic function in relation to the development of sexuality he describes what is effectively a universal operation. This complex topic will be developed by reference to a particular example of legal signification. The universal is founded on what 'negates' it. The woman's position in relation to the phallus is not the same as the man's. The man takes up the universal position of paternity by identifying with other men. Take, for instance, the idea of a legal right. These are essentially the rights of men. Feminists have pointed out that the historical declarations and catalogues of rights presuppose a male, rather than a female subject. To be a citizen is thus to be considered as like other male citizens, a bearer of certain inviolable rights that define your place. From this perspective, the contemporary problem has been to establish whether women are to be considered as similar or different. Should women be considered as bearers of the same catalogue of rights as men, or should there be specific rights that cover, for example, reproduction? A development of this problem can be found in the work of Salecl.[36] She argues that there are at least two 'logics'

[36] See Salecl, R., 'Rights in Psychoanalytical and Feminist Perspective' (1995) 16 *Cadozo Law Review* 1121–39. Salecl's argument returns to the antinomy opened by Kennedy, the tension between the individual and the group. She frames her argument in terms of 'universalism and particularism' (1136). Lacanian theory can help clarify the impasse of contemporary rights discourse. Both 'Neo-Kantian' and Foucauldian approaches are somewhat limited. Neo-Kantianism sees rights as a necessary 'regulative principle' that allows an idea of the 'justness' of any particular law. They are thus part of a universal discourse. Foucauldians would reject this idea of rights as already compromised by dominant power discourses. Any legal notion is too enmeshed in networks of power

available to articulate the law. The first 'male' logic would argue that all people have legal rights except those in excluded categories. 'Feminine' logic would suggest, alternatively, that all individuals bear rights, but that people, as a general category, do not have rights. This means that male logic stresses similarity, the inclusion of all people into general categories of rights bearers, whereas feminine logic stresses difference, or the need to respect the specificity of differently embodied people at the level of creating formal legal rights.

It is necessary to clarify the use of the terms 'female' and 'male' at this stage. These terms refer primarily to a sexuality that cannot be identified with gender. Male and female do not necessarily correspond with physically differentiated bodies. They are categories produced by the Lacanian logic of signification, referring, essentially to a relationship to the master signifier. Two consequences follow. First, it is possible to be a physical male with a female subjectivity, and secondly, and possibly more important here, there is a way of thinking, writing and feeling that is not directly subject to the dominant discourse. These implications need to be pursued. It is necessary to begin with the assertion that there can be no sexual relationship. This claim is as much about the logic of representation and signification as it is physical and emotional intimate attachments. One of the consequences of having language is to be forever separated from the other, unable to coincide with them. But this failure

to operate as a critical term. This tradition would stress the need to study particular situations and conflicts. Feminist theory also misunderstands the nature of the general notion of rights, as 'only when people were perceived as formally equal did sexual difference as such become thinkable' (1131). Rather than paper over the real difficulties, Salecl proposes Lacanian theory as a way of opening up the 'dilemma' of 'individual and group rights'. The major advantage of the logic described above is that it enables a discourse on rights, without losing sight of the 'social antagonisms' that can become lost at the analytical legal level. We do, however, remain trapped within the 'antinomies' of social existence. For further useful elaborations of Lacanian theory with reference to law, see Voruz, V., 'Legal Responsibility and the Law of Symbolization' (2000) 13 *International Journal for the Semiotics of Law* 133–58. An engaging application of Lacan to legal theory is Minkinnen, P., *Thinking Without Desire* (Oxford, Hart Publishing, 1999).

opens the space of relationship anyway; 'what makes up for' the (sexual) relationship begins from the impossibility of its 'taking place'.[37] Relationship, then, presupposes a greater dissonance where there can be no return to a resolution of the same and the other.

To bring the two consequences together: denying that a sexual relationship can take place seems to mean that men and women do not belong together in some general category, there is no all-inclusive universal from which all meaning can be plotted. As Salecl writes:'[w]oman . . . is in respect to the symbolic order not whole, as she is not totally bounded and determined by the phallic function'.[38] That woman is not whole means that she cannot be constituted by reference to a transcendental category. Consequently, there is something that can be related to women and their position in the symbolic order that enters language, but cannot be defined within language. To follow through this Lacanian formula would move towards the problematic notion of the real, that which resists and demands symbolisation. Where does this leave a critical theory of law?

Refer back to the developments of a feminine logic reviewed above. It suggests that the institution of the law is open to a different reading. If there is a critique of law it could begin with those moments when the logic of the law is disturbed or interrupted, when the real interrupts the symbolic order. Within Lacanian theory, the real occupies a complex position. At a therapeutic level it can be linked to the symptoms that are the speech of the unconscious. From the present perspective, the real is what will always return to the moment when an order of discourse is challenged by what it has no way of articulating. Thus, a symbolic order is never entirely coherent with the events of the world that it tries to describe. It may be the case that the interruption can be normalised, that the symbolic order can generate concepts or symbols to incorporate the anomaly and reduce its threat, but the threat can always return.

---

[37] Lacan, *supra* n. 23.
[38] *Ibid.*, 1135.

To carry forward the legacy of CLS, perhaps the most essential lesson is one of the uncertainties of legal concepts. This would return to the seminal moment of critique discussed above. One perceives the construction of the social world in moments of 'uncertainty', when the 'boundaries of legitimate rationality' are challenged.

The other essential factor would be that uncertainty is generated in the spaces that exist between people, in the social world that is both defined by law and constantly pushing against those definitions. The focus of law and aesthetics should be this problematic sense of fractured sociality.

However, as much as psychoanalysis can open the space of critique, is there a limitation to the insights that can be gained? Psychoanalysis risks the dependence of the subject on the analyst. For Lacan it is the 'power of practitioners' that can reveal to the analysand that 'thou art that'.[39] There would be no point in objecting to the power of the law to cede to the power of psychoanalysis. It may be the case that one has to work through psychoanalysis itself. The next chapter will suggest a working through of analysis, which does not stay completely within its terms of mastery.[40] This resonates with a further set of concerns that are linked to law and ethics. It returns to the question that haunted the aesthetic politics of CLS: how are we to live? Lacan describes as

[39] Lacan, *supra* n. 27, 7.

[40] It takes as its starting point Lacan's statement: 'there is a danger in a public discourse, precisely in so far as it is addressed to those nearest—Nietzsche knew this, a certain type of discourse can be addressed only to those furthest away' see *The Four Fundamental Concepts of Psychoanalysis* (London, Penguin, 1977), 23. For a broader critique of Lacan and Legendre, see Douzinas, C., *Law and the Emotions: Prolegomena for a Psychoanalytic Approach to Legal Study* (San Domenico, EUI Working Paper no. 98/9: Badia Fiesolana, 1988) 18–23: '[a] critical jurisprudence must question the conservative repercussions of his judicial anthropology' (18). In this reading, Legendre is associated with the negative Catholic reaction to modernity. From a critical perspective, Legendre's relevance is his style of thinking, his recovery of a judicial logic that contributes to law's hold over the social world. Alain Pottage's 'The Paternity of Law' in Douzinas *et al.* (eds.), *Politics, Postmodernity and Critical Legal Studies* (London, Routledge, 1994), 147–87, opposes the work of the French scholar Luce Irigaray to Legendre as a more progressive articulation of a critical appropriation of psychoanalysis.

'scandalous' the commandment to love one's neighbour as oneself (*Tu aimeras ton prochain comme toi-même*). The English obscures the sense in which there is a play here on the notion that the neighbour is the one that is closest to you. It seems that a working through of the psychoanalytic must then concern an ethics that is addressed to the one both closest and, paradoxically, most far away. The Christian context of the commandment suggests further lines of enquiry. It is a law that one encounters in the world in a specific and frightening moment when everything is at stake. It will be argued that these concerns are brought together by a Nietzschean discourse that negotiates aesthetics and ethics.

Against the command of the analyst, 'thou art that', there is the imperative of the aesthetic: 'Be Yourself'.

Coda

One of the seminal texts of CLS was an exchange between Duncan Kennedy and Peter Gabel published in the *Harvard Law Review*. This text appeared as a dialogue rather than a conventional essay, a form that suited the attempt to discover a kind of sociality that resists definition. In Gabel's formulation, we are 'separate and together'.[41] Could this be reclaimed by a space of critique opened by psychoanalysis?[42] Rather than writing criticism of Gabel and Kennedy's dialogue, it might be best to try and continue it. The very title of the article, 'Roll Over Beethoven', taken from Chuck Berry's song of the same name, suggests that this dialogue is one concerned with succession, with the continuation of a style, with starting anew. The following dialogue imagines a spirit of continuation:

Student: CLS represented a new beginning, and that is good. But it is now associated with the baggage of ideologies and the old world that are no longer any use for us now. Moreover, you didn't change the world.

---

[41] Gabel and Kennedy, n. 5 *supra*, 14.

[42] See William MacNeil *Law's Corpus Delicti: the Fantasmatic Body of Rights Discourse, Law and Critique* 9, (1998), 37.57.

Professor: Are you saying that we should stop reading Marx, or Sartre or Heidegger? Or is it a question of trying again? Reading them differently? CLS cannot, ultimately, be seen in narrow terms as the replacement of the law—rather it is a form of cultural critique that borrows from crisis and uncertainty. CLS is a politics of the everyday.

Student: OK—but it seemed to do this from a kind of Marxist total theory, a complete description of the world. Although certain critical scholars developed theories of law that resisted a class analysis, I feel that law's functioning cannot be explained in such reductivist terms.

Professor: Firstly, it would be wrong to say that CLS was simply Marxist. Secondly, Marx's myth is too dangerous to believe in, and too important to jettison completely. You will have to make your peace with his ghost.

Student: It seems to me that CLS should not itself become rigid or reified in a certain moment. Surely this was the point of the discussion in 'Roll Over Beethoven'; formulations such as the 'essential contradiction', 'intersubjective zap' were approximations, they were not gospel. The major problem now seems to be that your thought looks for a moment of purity: an unreified consciousness, a point from which we can start again. I do not think that is available. It's far too hippy. The golden age has gone. Woodstock turned into Baader-Meinhof.

Professor: So what is the alternative? Old age and cynicism? It is the duty of every generation to define its golden age. That responsibility is more acute if you see yourself as oppositional.

Student: Oppositional? Do you mean that there is an 'outside' to the law?

Professor: There are various 'outsides' already within the law. You run the risk of pretending that the law is more monolithic than it is. There is always the possibility that the law can be changed from within, that legal strategies can be developed. But I am talking at a philosophical level as well. By oppositional I mean at least you don't like Dworkin or Rawls, at most that you find in yourself a strange mixture of pessimism and optimism and that you feel, as you told me, that we have to try again.

Besides, the moment of purity, the golden age, is, in your own terms, just an approximation. You have to keep looking. The golden age might be the very search itself. It is active, a process. Your own language is deceiving you.

Student: OK. If we look at reification, and that seems a key term for your movement, it appears to me that it is our condition of being and thought in a sense more profound than you would allow. It is not simply a question of a social movement, or a revolution that can sweep it away and replace it with a purer community. We need to discover the extent to which we can still act authentically within reification.

Professor: If I accept the idea of CLS as a movement in search for a theory, then I could go along with this.

Student: Do you think the aesthetic could provide a starting point? Perhaps we need to look again at the way in which images hold us, but we can also become images for ourselves: we can become our own work.

Professor: Sounds like you've been reading Nietzsche.

Student: Spot on professor. This would be true to the ideas of CLS in a way, the need to look outside of Anglo-American jurisprudence—to reinvent; we could also look again at your rather sketchy application of psychoanalysis to the image. Perhaps you need to work on yourself, change yourself before you can even begin to think of working on the world.

Professor: Or as a way of working on the world?

3

The Book of Sand
Nietzsche and Aesthetic Responsibility

'The sober, the weary, the dried up (e.g. scholars) can receive absolutely nothing from art, because they do not possess the primary artistic force, the pressure of abundance: whosoever cannot give also receives nothing.'

> Nietzsche, F., *The Will to Power* (New York, Vintage, 1968) 422.[1]

Supposing that it were possible to learn anything from Nietzsche, one might take the following lesson. The law rests upon an unsure foundation. Law embodies a form, a set of values that mandate a way of living. What allows the law to be posited in the first place could also perhaps lead to its overcoming. One would require sufficient desire to will the law anew. Aesthetics is, at heart, this energy to mandate the form of a world, to create oneself. Ultimately it is the courage to will an ethics, to take from the law its power to determine forms of community. A notebook fragment gives a sense of this all-consuming need to adopt responsibility: '[h]ow lightly one takes the burden of an excuse upon oneself, so long as one has to be responsible for nothing. BUT I AM ACCOUNTABLE'.[2] One has to adopt an accountability *to* oneself for what one is or what one could become. But this is not a solipsism. The ideas of eternal recurrence, the will

---

[1] This chapter owes a debt to Jacques Derrida's reading of friendship in *The Politics of Friendship* (London, Verso, 1997).

[2] Quoted in Waite, G., *Nietzsche's Corpse* (Durham, N.C., Duke University Press, 1996), 395. Waite is quoting from Colli, G., Montinari, M. (eds.), *Kritische Gesamtausgabe, Werke* (Berlin, Walter de Gruyter, 1967), 7/1: 383.

to power and Zarathustra's doctrine of friendship will be taken as a sustained meditation and transformation of the command to love the other as yourself; the new law appearing from the husk of the old.

Nietzsche amongst the theorists

At the start of this chapter it is necessary to clarify some preliminary issues. Nietzsche is a notoriously difficult writer. This difficulty stems more from the style than the content of his thought and has led to the myriad interpretations of his work. Although the secondary literature cannot properly be reviewed here, there is still an obligation to outline and defend the approach that is to be developed.

Nietzsche is most commonly associated with the thesis that, as God is dead, everything can be justified and nothing is forbidden. In a more sophisticated version, this is extended to mean that it is no longer possible to ground thought. Any truth claim is contestable as there is no overarching and universally accepted standard of verification. These interpretations are not uninformed, but they do need to be clarified. To paraphrase Gillian Rose,[3] Nietzsche's critical 'project' begins with an identification of philosophy as a grounding of morality. Morality is not just one aspect of the world, it is the very imposition of reality. Thus to criticise the constitution of morality is to initiate a reappraisal of the very way in which thought makes the world. In the face of the authority of morality, 'one is not allowed to think, far less to express an opinion: here one has to obey!'[4] For Nietzsche, the questioning of the law opens a contradiction between the laws of morality and a 'thou shalt', or 'the last moral law' whose imperative was 'to live'.[5] In the place of the law of truth is the obligation to create. To 'refound' thought there is an obligation

---

[3] Rose, G., *The Melancholic Science: An Introduction to the Thought of Theodor W. Adorno* (London, Macmillan, 1978) 18.

[4] Nietzsche, F., *Daybreak* (Cambridge, Cambridge University Press, 1982), 2.

[5] *Ibid.*, 2.

to move away from what is 'outlived and decayed' whilst acknowledging that what remains in the decayed form is the spark of a force that once had a foundational energy.

Although this way of reading raises the spectre of indeterminacy, this thesis should not be overstated. Thought is indeterminate for Nietzsche to the extent that any foundational claim can be contested by a critical activity that scrutinises what has been and imagines what is to come. This cannot be co-ordinated with a wholehearted rejection of any standards of thought, although it is difficult to describe exactly what is to be preserved and what is to be rejected. What can most safely be said is that Nietzsche's thought would seek to problematise and destroy a certain idea of social scientific enquiry. Associated with nineteenth-century modes of enquiry in the natural and social sciences, this thinking tended to study phenomena in a disconnected way. It took for granted social structures that were merely contingent and lent them a 'semblance of necessity and authority',[6] or it searched for 'rules' of historical progress and saw events as somehow fitting into more or less determined patterns. To attack these forms of scientific thought is not to reject the possibility of any form of enquiry that seeks to make and justify claims about the world. After all, the gay science is the art of observation, a chemistry of the moral sensations, addressing the 'agitations we experience within ourselves in cultural and social intercourse'.[7]

The gay science, then, is not a rejection of reason or argument. As has been pointed out, this argument is largely sustained by a misidentification of what is claimed for reason either through an ignorance of particular philosophies, or a willful identification of rationalist philosophies with absurdly grand claims about the nature of reason. If the gay science is a chemistry of our emotions and sensations, and its questioning is to be

[6] Unger, R., *Social Theory* (Cambridge, Cambridge University Press, 1987), 2.

[7] Nietzsche, F., *The Gay Science* (New York, Vintage, 1974). In this chapter, and in the remainder of the book, the gay science will also refer to the four books, *Daybreak, Human All Too Human, The Gay Science* and *Thus Spake Zarathustra* considered collectively.

seen as integral to a jurisprudence, then there would be no profound disagreement from the champions of reasoned discourse.
Reason can be applied to 'one's beliefs, or emotions, or attitudes, or actions, as the case may be'.[8] Moreover, contemporary
legal thought does not depend on foundationalist claims. Indeed,
reason can exist alongside the paradoxes that have always troubled those who seek to provide a thorough philosophical ground.
Paradoxes may 'challenge the coherence of reason'[9] in all its
fundamental categories, 'it would take a brave man to say that
they were all solved successfully'. But these failures are of no real
concern to the endeavour. People have not stopped thinking
rationally simply because there were contradictions within
rational thought. Indeed, one possible explanation is that reason
is itself 'incoherent and self contradictory'. We are condemned

---

[8] See Gardner, J., and Macklem, T., in Coleman, J., and Shapiro, S., *The
Oxford Handbook of Jurisprudence* (Oxford, OUP, forthcoming 2001).

[9] Raz, J., *Engaging Reason* (Oxford, Oxford University Press, 1999), 80. In
this work there is a brief discussion of Nietzsche and the aesthetic. Raz could be
read as suggesting that aesthetic criteria are as much occasions for revolt over
supposed shared standards as determination of objective standards of universal
application. This does not, however, deny the possibility of reasoned discussion.
Raz asks how can one compare the value of a novel and a poem? It may, of
course, be more or less possible to compare different novels and different poems.
There are standards that are generated by 'social practices' and by the criteria
of judgement they promulgate. But this would not allow different orders or distinct values to be compared. If there are 'inherent' (at 195) standards, they do
not properly allow distinct practices to be compared as the 'rankings' that they
supposedly generate are too 'fragile'. Rather than universal criteria, they are in
turn riven by 'tensions', disputes over their composition, and hence could as
much be criteria of revolt from existing standards as they are points of objective
determination. However, if one is to allow this plurality of value, one does not
have to accept the 'incommensurabililty of reasons' (at 196). Reasons for aesthetic
choices can be seen as stemming not from values but from 'taste' or 'ambition'.
These reference points allow arguments that are reasonable. For example, an
individual's taste for a particular writer is reason enough without attempting to
rank this writing alongside that of other writers: it is reasonable to allow this to
'guide . . . actions and commitments' (at 196). Raz's only reference to Nietzsche
occurs in this context: Nietzsche was 'primarily concerned to contrast the aesthetic with the moral point of view' (at 264). The argument in this chapter is,
on the contrary, Nietzsche connects ethics and aesthetics.

to continue to think rationally. A more extended conclusion is possible. If the doctrines of reason are contradictory, if the 'cogency of . . . concepts' and 'rules of inference' are not sustainable, it does not follow that the 'possibility of reason' is itself jettisoned. 'Formal reason' survives the maelstrom.[10] The manifesto for reason's survival would suggest that substantive doctrines can be challenged and can be modified. It would refute the conventional belief that reason rests on timeless a priori principles. The most minimal condition is that 'we are capable of being normatively guided'.[11]

How can this be developed? Referring back to Rose's point above, Nietzsche can be seen as discovering an ethical imperative that precipitates claims about the need to invent a code of values. This is the primary obligation of the superman. Whether or not these values co-ordinate with the values that have taken the form of a law commanding obedience is a second issue. Addressing this latter point is a difficult task that will extend over the next two chapters. Indeed one of the problems with arguing the relevance of Nietzsche's thought to contemporary law is that, whereas it can orientate thought to a notion of creativity, it lacks a thorough engagement with the idea and practice of the legal institution. An aesthetic jurisprudence drawing on Nietzsche also tends to draw on a set of concepts and a language alien to Anglo-American legal thought. Mending the breach, creating any kind of dialogue would have to contend with a complex set of conjunctures and disjunctures between two different traditions. Although not impossible, it would demand a larger book than this one.

The present chapter, then, must be read in a more exploratory and preliminary sense. It will present Nietzsche as a pioneer who enables a thinking about law that will be developed in the remainder of this book. So far it has been argued that the human subject is 'alienated' or divided from the world and a legal aesthetics takes this as its starting point. Psychoanalysis has been presented as one way to come to terms with this alienation,

[10] *Ibid.*, 82.
[11] *Ibid.*, 89.

preventing the self from being crushed by the weight of existence. After analysis, the subject becomes responsible for his or her self. At the same time, as was urged in the previous chapter, it is necessary to be in touch with psychoanalysis without being in its thrall. Against the claims of the psychoanalysts, a Nietzschean aesthetic responsibility will be proposed. First, mythology must be rescued from psychoanalysis; it is then necessary to see how the Nietzschean text performs the very aesthetic responsibility that it describes.

The tragic sense of life: becoming responsible for the fiction of the self

The tragic sense of life is an articulation of the subject as an interpreter of his or her self.

Understanding this fundamental aspect of the human condition means returning to its first articulation in Greek dramatic art, the problem of human finitude as evoked in the myth of Silenus:

> An old legend has it that King Midas hunted a long time in the woods for the wise Silenus, companion of Dionysos, without being able to catch him. When he finally caught him the king asked him what he considered man's greatest good. The daemon remained sullen and uncommunicative until finally, forced by the king, he broke into a shrill laugh and spoke: 'Ephemeral wretch, begotten by accident and toil, why do you force me to tell you what it would be your greatest boon not to hear? What would be best for you is quite beyond your reach: not to have been born, not to be, to be nothing. But the second best is to die soon.'[12]

Silenus' answer can be read as a poetic articulation of the same problem that psychoanalysis attempts to resolve. The problem of being is that one is separated from the dumb vital power of nature, the human subject is alienated in its very being by consciousness. Like King Midas one is condemned to being. Life was bearable for the Greeks because they created gods. In *The Birth of Tragedy*, this invention of gods is linked to the urge to

---

[12] Nietzsche, F., *The Birth of Tragedy* (New York, Anchor, 1956), 29.

create. Although the urge expressed itself primarily as the need to create gods, it is more properly the art of creating the self. Gods represent the potentialities of the self. One has to assume this primal artistic responsibility for oneself. Learnt from the tragic art of the Greeks is thus an art of becoming human. Their fictions still speak to us, especially the tension represented by the two gods Apollo and Dionysus.

The Apollonian element of art demands that the artist take responsibility for images and their possible effects. Apollo is the god of light and vision. Opposed to the Apollonian is the Dionysian. The Dionysian goes beyond the individual towards some kind of communication with a world of wider instincts. Dionysus evokes the reversal; the world turned upside down, the carnival, unruly and formless energy. His rites could destroy the individual. Dionysian frenzy could become the blind worship of energy. At worst, the Dionysian is an insight into an energy that does not care for consciousness. As a destruction of the established laws of the tribe, it is the liberation of the aggression and anti-social desires that those laws might have restrained. In its benign aspect, however, the Dionysian is the golden age returned, nature appearing reconciled with man in an earthly paradise. How is Dionysus to be invoked in his benign aspect?

Dionysian energy has both a positive and a negative aspect. How could the artist know that an act of creation would invoke the utopian aspect, rather than the destructive frenzy? Imposing too rigid an interpretation on what this archaeology has unearthed would be foolish. It would be wrong to describe the Dionysian as the unconscious and the Apollonian as conscious order as this would be simply to impose the terms of one discourse upon another. It should not be necessary to relate these fictions back to the Oedipus complex. Tragic art was not used up in analysis; it became creative, producing dramatic myths that were enacted for an audience. The argument here, however, will be more precise. If it is possible to suggest that tragedy makes life bearable as an aesthetic phenomenon, the aesthetic in a broader sense is a discourse about a creative will to interpret the personal and communal circumstances of existence. If this work has anything to offer the law, it is the sense in which legal thought must become creative. This moves towards the idea of an ethics that is provoked by the desire to articulate the primary urge of law: the articulation of community, the need to live with others. The first step in the argument is to show that interpretation involves a question of responsibility, the artist must achieve an Apollonian insight into the act of creation.

It is a question of becoming responsible for one's representations. To press energy into form, the artist must invoke Apollo. Calling on Apollo demands that the supplicant is aware of a peculiar ethical prerogative:

> As a moral deity Apollo demands self control from his people and, in order to observe such control, a knowledge of self.[13]

It is important to understand the conditional nature of this discussion of the normative. Introducing this paragraph on the demands of Apollo is a conditional sentence. 'If this apotheosis of individuation is to be read in normative terms . . .' '[I]f' normative terms are introduced, this particular notion of an ethics of self might be supposed. Ultimately, this 'if' has no source, no guarantee outside itself; it is rooted in the human response to the tragedy of life. If one is to adopt responsibility for one's life as an aesthetic phenomenon, then it rests on nothing other than the duty one adopts towards oneself and one's creation.

The most frightening moment is willing the ethical 'if' for oneself. Willing the 'if' is frightening because one becomes god-like, or one assumes the creative 'power' that was represented in the form of a god. Responsibility for what one will *become* is adopted through an act of will. This would be the first lesson of the gay science.

The second lesson of the gay science shows that the act of reading is an exemplification of the art of becoming, which is the adoption of responsibility for one's interpretations. A reader's response to the text is a figure of the adoption of aesthetic responsibility itself. Although a complex process, it can be approached in the following way. Nietzsche's text appears as something that

---

[13] Nietzsche, F., *The Birth of Tragedy* (New York, Anchor, 1956), 34.

constantly returns to itself and comments upon its own return, its own re-reading of itself. This both anticipates those readings that are to come and places them in a series of readings that the text has itself initiated. Potentially infinite, this process is a figuring of creative activity. At the level of any individual text, or indeed throughout the *œuvre*, this interpretative happening can be observed at many levels. A reader could discover it in the repetition of certain themes, the injunctions to the reader, or the questionings that recur in the text. To aid in the demonstration of this concern, the key figure of the book will be focused upon.

The book can only ever become 'almost human', an implicit warning against believing in the purity of text. Only people, the interpreters of texts, can become. So, the 'best author is ashamed to become a writer'[14] because the best author is concerned with himself or herself as a work of art. As much as art can tell us about self-becoming, it cannot replace it because becoming cannot be identified with any one goal. The book itself becomes 'detached'[15] from the writer. Once the book has been written, it belongs to its readers. In the eyes of these readers, it 'engenders new works', amazes and terrifies. Just as the author is not important, the discourses of genius and inspiration that grow up around the names of great artists obscure a form of bad faith. One might even have to be flippant towards claims of genius. Cults of genius deny the innate powers of any individual to become an artist. In place of this cult, there is the truth of the 'serious workman' [but remember that nothing human can be treated with too much seriousness]. The point is 'to acquire greatness', to give oneself the time and the distance to become an artist.[16] This is why another aphorism denies the originality of art.[17] Art must not slavishly utilise old forms, it must endlessly perform the act of its own definition.

---

[14] Nietzsche, F., *Human All Too Human* (Cambridge, Cambridge University Press, 1986), 93.

[15] *Ibid.*, 97.

[16] Science is the process of creating incrementally, of observing the local and the transient. It is part of the work of becoming, and in this sense linked to art.

[17] Nietzsche, n. 14 *supra*, 92.

Towards this end it is best to imagine the text of *The Gay Science* as a series of voices asserting, counter-asserting, arguing, singing and shouting. It could be said that this is the impossibility of discourse. There is no coherent development of theme, no movement from hypothesis to conclusion. A reader is forced to chose and will a reading, to adopt a responsibility towards a reading of the text. A comparison is invited with the texts of Shakespeare. Shakespeare was 'incapable' of discourse: 'instead he placed observations *about* the passions into the mouths of impassioned characters'.[18] The 'repugnance' that this can arouse in the audience is similar to that occasioned by Nietzsche's own work. The latter conflates the representation of a position by a character or a voice with the voice of the author himself. One searches in vain for moral co-ordinates that would allow the truth to be sifted from error. The voices, the characters that appear, all want to impose themselves on your reading consciousness. They all want to tell you the truth.

Who are you going to listen to? Can you assume responsibility for your own truth?

The reader has to become a writer of the work and to take responsibility for a reading. So, how would one read the law? A contemporary reader might find this thinking far too abstract and remote. Where is the examination of legal doctrine, the discussion of case law or legal institutions? Chapter 5 will attempt to remedy this problem. At present the engagement is with a different, but related problem. Nietzsche is interrogating the foundations of law, an approach that necessarily demands an engagement with history, mythology and theology. It is in these forms of knowledge and practice that law has its roots. This is a question of origins. Why should law emerge in the first place? There are a host of connected questions. What are the conditions of its emergence, and what is at stake when it does appear? How does law affect the way people conceive of themselves? Is the law necessarily a fixed form, compelling allegiance, or does

[18] Nietzsche, n. 14 *supra*, 91.

the law contain its own overturning? Can there be any resistance to the idea of law, or is the human soul always implicated, forever trapped in the need either to obey an existing code, or to create a rival code anew? *The Gay Science* offers itself as a resource to the philosophical adventurer tackling these questions.

Weights and measures

When did the law come into being? If one were to trace law's origin, one would find that it was coeval with the discovery of 'weights and measures' and the very idea of man. Indeed, Nietzsche derives the word Man from *Mensch*, the measurer.[19] This cryptic etymology discovers the very source of measure as that which exceeds the possibility of measurement.[20] Measure leads to realms 'that are quite unmeasurable and unweighable, but originally did not seem to be'.[21] In a compressed, cryptic form, this expresses the relationship between the creative one and the law. Rules fetishise. The creative one must be able to link the form of the law to a new content. There is always a struggle between form and what exceeds form.

To fathom this problem, to engage with the question of an interpretative and a physical violence, one needs to return to an earlier age and confront the figure of the lawmaker. In comparison with an earlier 'mode of life', the time of the lawmaker, the contemporary appears most impoverished. The hold of morality and custom over the soul and the imagination is now almost completely dissipated. Any question of violence has been forgotten. This is why the assessment of morality as no more than obedience to customs appears in itself inadequate to modern minds. But this proposition does carry an insight.

If one accounts for morality as the obligation to abide by tradition then the 'free individual' who 'determines' their own values is 'immoral' because he or she lives apart from tradition.

[19] *Ibid.*, at 310.
[20] *Ibid.*, at 311.
[21] *Ibid.*

In this rude state, 'evil signifies the same as "individual", "free", "capricious", "unusual", "unforeseen", "incalculable" '.[22] Tradition thus appears as a 'higher authority'[23] whose 'commands' are 'obeyed'. Strictly the individual has no place in this order. A later meditation explains how even apparently ridiculous customs, such as forbidding the 'impaling of coal on a knife', serve to keep in the consciousness of the individual the tradition itself. Keeping the tradition in mind is the perpetuation of ordered social life.[24] Any question of values that are 'useful' to the individual cannot be grasped because custom is the source of social life and hence largely invisible. However, if one again contemplates the 'free individual' it might be appreciated that this understanding of tradition is inadequate.

Any set of customs may, more precisely, reflect a 'set of motives which founded the tradition'.[25] The lawgiver has to 'elevate' himself/herself above the tradition to mandate new laws and customs. There is bound to be tension between the old and the new law. Plato, as a lawgiver, threatened the community as his doctrines urged people to consider custom and usage from the perspective of reason. Plato was condemned to death. The ambivalence towards Plato is repeated in the Roman attitude to Christianity. Roman disdain for Christianity is hostility towards a belief in personal salvation that can put the individual in opposition to the political community. The violence with which the Romans persecuted the early Christians is thus the physical reflex of a system of ideas and beliefs that felt challenged by something that seemed to move beyond it. Violence, then, is as much a symbolic or interpretative phenomenon as physical force. A new interpretation performs a kind of violence on any opposed view. Taken to its extreme, a particularly radical interpretation could invalidate everything that comes before it. In Chapter 5, the implications of this understanding will be elaborated in a consideration of contemporary legal doctrine, but further considerations

[22] Nietzsche, n.4 *supra*, 10.
[23] *Ibid.*, at 9.
[24] *Ibid.*, at 16.
[25] *Ibid.*, at 10.

of this problem in this chapter would obscure the questions posed by *The Gay Science*.

Interpretative violence is linked to the very possibility of Nietzsche's own thought. His problematic is that of the resources for his own critique of Christianity. These are great and terrible themes, which can only be touched upon here. If one were to trace this genealogy, one would first have to account for the violent emergence of Christianity from Judaism. To some extent, this theme has already entered into and influenced critical legal thought. *Ressentiment*, the reaction of the Christians to the heroic ethic of the Old Testament, becomes a way of thinking the legal mind itself.[26] But this approach can only be partial if Nietzsche's relationship to Christianity is not studied. Once again, though, this necessitates sketching the contour of a much grander and more terrible theme. Running through these rejections of dominant world views is the discovery of the explosive one, the interrupter, who realises that it is only as an aesthetic phenomenon that the world can be justified. In different ways: Socrates, Caesar and Napoleon. Christ is a special case. He is the exemplar and the one who destroys the example.[27] The explosive one destroys an old order in the foundation of the new. Over-determining the different politics and theologies of revolutionary activity is the notion of aesthetic responsibility. To remain in the thrall of an old order is to act with a bad conscience. One must take upon oneself the creative power to fashion a world and create a table of values, to 'realise the weights of all things must be determined anew'.[28] The aphorism that states 'you shall become the person that you are'[29] celebrates this power to determine, this will to create. Just as poets are responsible for gods, men can generate their own possibilities.

[26] See Weisberg, R., *The Failure of the Word* (New Haven Conn., Yale University Press, 1984).

[27] This is why Christ unsettles Nietzsche so much; and why, in some senses, Dionysus is the crucified. See Nietzsche, F., *Ecce Homo* (London, Penguin, 1979), 134.

[28] Nietzsche, n. 14 *supra*, 218.

[29] *Ibid.*

Thus, to trace the emergence of the law is to discover conflict. Any code of values determined by a religion or a philosophy can be overturned. Thinking in this way is problematic, as it tends to personalise history and obscure the complex factors that allow thought to emerge. In defence, it might be suggested that it tends towards striking and poetic expression rather than historical verisimilitude. Allow for a moment that Niezsche has discovered a 'truth' that is as relevant for our jurisprudence as it was for the emergence of the more ancient forms of thought actually discussed. The provocation could be explained as follows: how does contemporary law contain its own overcoming? To accept the Nietzschean imperative, the legal philosopher would have to discover both the possibility of law's reinvention, and then take a responsibility for the new forms that he or she sought to nurture. But how could this new law, this counter-law, be imagined? Surely simply showing that law will always tend towards its overcoming is a philosophy of chaos and despair that could hardly be recommended. The following section will suggest that authentic reinvention of codes of value is done in the name of a profound urge to ethics.

The explosive one must will an ethics.

Neighbour, stranger, lover, friend

The Gay Science is a treatise on ethics, an examination of how we are to live with others. To study oneself, one must be prepared to suspend the old certainties about moral behaviour. The great critique of Christian morality that runs through the *œuvre* can be read as a radical examination, not a rejection, of an ethical relation to the other. As they stand, the virtues cannot be considered ethical because they stem from an impoverished spirit. What is attacked is not so much the value itself, but how it is presented, how the 'teachers' of morality sponsor a particular social vision. Ethical values can be recuperated, but not before they have been made problematic. Consider the virtue of neighbourliness, the great injunction to treat the other as you would yourself, that lies at the heart of Christianity.

How is this central ethical principle to be 're-valued'? The problem is, first, that considering the injunction independently of context can destroy its meaning. Nietzsche's critique operates by considering how the injunction can be misused, turned against itself, when it becomes a 'general' social value. When virtue is considered good from the perspective of society, from the viewpoint of its utility, the individual is integrated into the whole, his or her good is sacrificed for that of society at large. Once it is recommended by the socially powerful that 'you shall renounce yourself and sacrifice yourself', the original injunction is destroyed.[30] It could only be preached as a social value if the proponents of morality themselves renounced their own advantage. This is not to argue that the injunction should be rejected, but to major in the gay science is to become aware that its transformation from a statement of altruism into a social mores could destroy any real ethical value. Only where a certain exuberance is practiced might any ethical value be recovered. To love one's neighbour, one would have to renounce oneself. The work on the self cannot proceed without some account being taken of this authentic morality.

It is necessary to see this opposition to utility as part of a wider critique of any kind of religious value that adopts an 'economy' of exchange. Thus, in place of the traditional Christian command to honour the giver, there is the need for a certain ungratefulness that remains true to the logic of giving. To give, one has to relinquish all hope of a return; gratitude cannot be the motive for giving. Pity and compassion must also be recuperated. Pity in some contexts could be ethically worthless. What is the value, for instance, of the tyrant's pity? To be grateful for pity in this context is to devalue moral language. To accept pity in this case would be the same as exchanging the coins of a devalued currency. One has to begin from the position that 'benefiting and hurting others are ways of exercising one's power'.[31] As commentators have pointed out, this represents the beginnings of the

[30] Nietzsche, n. 7 *supra*, 94.
[31] *Ibid.*, 86.

65

will to power, and this ethical orientation must be remembered when this is discussed later in this chapter. To benefit someone means that they become grateful to you; the gift returns to the giver, our sense of power is increased. It is a question of 'how one is accustomed to *spice* one's life',[32] a problem of 'temperament'. In other words, these ethical problems can be related back only to the aesthetic work upon oneself. It is part of the need to 'give style' to oneself, an 'art' that is expressed in terms of what is 'needful'.[33] As a necessary response to the ambiguities of life 'strengths and weaknesses' cannot be considered in absolute terms. They have to be fitted into an 'artistic plan' that balances them against each other.

Nietzsche's articulation of this 'balancing' rests on a reinterpretation of the original Christian concern with 'love of our neighbor'.[34] The difficulty is one of its 'doctrinal' presentation. The discourse of love has come from a particular history: 'linguistic usage has evidently been formed by those who did not possess but desired'.[35] Now the task is to possess and desire. The laughter of eros that introduces this task suggests the transforming spirit of gaiety and the coming of the superman. Although this is a break, it is also 'a kind of continuation of love' where the possessive urge becomes a new '*shared* higher thirst' that is not somehow coherent and identifiable with the relationship of the lovers, but is somehow 'above them'. To possess desire is to have this higher thirst. This 'ideal' can be named and experienced. It is 'friendship'. Friendship, described as 'the law *above* us', establishes an important link between the higher thirst of love and the law. Understanding means approaching the doctrine of Zarathustra and the much maligned and misunderstood notion of the will to power.

---

[32] Nietzsche, n. 7 *supra*, 87.
[33] *Ibid.*, 232.
[34] *Ibid.*, 88.
[35] *Ibid.*, 89.

Zarathustra's doctrine: the law of friendship and the will to power

Will to power is connected with ethics and the law as it expresses itself as a source of ethical evaluation. Evaluation expresses itself as the ability to ascribe good and evil. There are a number of aspects of this notion. Will to power is an ontology that presents the essence of the human as the need to evaluate the world. It presupposes that human will is all there is after the death of God. Just as the subject is condemned to being, the will to power condemns the human to evaluation. This, of course, presupposes language, and, indeed, the will to power is also the ability to 'conceive' all being. One can perceive here the correspondence between will to power and the weights and measures of the law. Will may be the power to interpret the world, but this is based on a desire to '*make* all being conceivable'.[36] Strength of will is the ability to realise this constant force of reinvention, to be able to say 'I am that which must overcome itself again and again'.[37] It is this 'again and again' that will link will to power irretrievably to eternal recurrence, but before this is expanded, the dynamic must be observed in the development of the will to power itself.

This ontology, then, would find the obligation to evaluate the first problem in philosophy. It is a way of accounting for both individual will and the definition of a people as those who are under a law that they have given themselves: 'a table of values hangs over every people. Behold, it is the table of its overcomings; behold, it is the voice of its will to power'.[38] Values are, first, the structure that holds a community together. They are the 'tables of values' that 'hang over' a people. This verb describes an impending fate. Once again, we encounter the problem of the explosive one. There is something about evaluation that is inherently destructive. Precisely because man is an evaluator, the need to create new values endangers the community. Value is simultaneously a site of

---

[36] Nietzsche, F., *Thus Spake Zarathustra* (Penguin, London, 1961), 24.

[37] *Ibid.*, 138.

[38] *Ibid.*, 84.

solidarity and the overcoming of this into new expressions. To return to the language of the second chapter, desire is productive because it will never settle with one fantasmatic version of the law: 'a change in values—that means a change in the creators of values. He who has to be a creator always has to destroy'.[39]

Zarathustra's argument presents three examples of a people under the law. The examples are the Greeks, the Jews and the Germans. The argument is best glimpsed from the consideration of Jewish law. The Ten Commandments are summarised as follows: 'honour father and mother and [to] do their will even from the roots of the soul'.[40] This interpretation is not received from God, but from the human ability to evaluate. Soul, here, is more properly understood as the innermost site of the self that is the will to power. But there is an immediate agon to this evaluative activity. Zarathustra holds that no people wish to evaluate as their neighbours evaluate. This is in part a logic of the law. If the law founds a people, it must do so by exclusion, by making one community different from another. But this activity, if looked at historically, cannot just be linked with the formation of peoples. The modern problem is that the individual is the most recent creation. Zarathustra himself represents this most troubling invention which intensifies the problem of law and interpretation. Whereas the will to power expressed itself as the formation of communities that subordinated the individual to the law, the birth of the individual as interpreter makes for spectacular problems. The thousand and one goals are an expression of this problem. Zarathustra must contend with what is closest to him, those relationships with others that tradition has attempted to speak for and control and which only now can be properly perceived. The interpreter cannot refer back to the codes of the past, she or he must start again and determine the social world anew.

Will to power expresses itself in Zarathustra's doctrine of friendship. The friend intervenes in the loneliness of the self. Although loneliness is necessary, it needs to be interrupted:

---

[39] Nietzsche, F., *Thus Spake Zarathustra* (Penguin, London, 1961), 85.
[40] *Ibid.*, 85.

I and Me are always too earnestly in conversation with one another: how could it be endured if there was not a friend.[41]

The friend is the interlocutor, the one engaged in dialogue with the self. 'I and Me' suggests the reflexivity, the necessary sense in which one has to become an object of study for oneself. 'Me' appears here as the object of the 'I' but this relationship is constituted in 'conversation' and thus should not be seen as essential. They are, rather, positions that can be adopted. The relationship to the friend is a matter of difficulty. When the friend interrupts the conversation with the self, s/he does so not to support the self's comforting fictions. The true friend has to appear as an enemy. Indeed, the friend must steadfastly resist the friend. Although a reflection of the self, his 'face a rough and imperfect mirror'[42] he must remain 'near to' rather than be identical with the self. Proximity is a defining distance.

An ethic of friendship is a product of a history of moral sensations. Zarathustra's thinking addresses a particular moment. The problem with ethical expressions to date is the non-existence of an adequate language. Returning to the central commandment to 'love one's neighbour', the re-evaluator faces a complex problem. Not least is a variation of what interrupts the hermit's meditations: 'the you is older than the I'.[43] The ethical situation is that of the priority of the other. Not only is this a feature of the ethical codes that speak in terms of duties to others, but the temporal chronology can also be understood as an existential dilemma. As the hermit finds, the conversation with the other is necessary to the dialogue with the self. The existence of the other is not only inseparable from the appearance of the self, but is somehow prior. 'You' is in this sense 'consecrated'. If the doctrine of the superman is to become what one already is, then this return to a primal relation with the enemy/friend is central to becoming. The consecration of the 'I' can take place only in an ethical language that can articulate this simultaneous

[41] *Ibid.*, 82.
[42] *Ibid.*, 81.
[43] *Ibid.*, 86.

return and advance. It is a language of exhortation: '[d]o I exhort you to love of your neighbor? I exhort you rather to flight from your neighbor and to the love of the most distant.'[44] A distance must separate contemporary ethical terms from what they will become.

Zarathustra describes the distance as love. But this has to be read as an approximation, for virtue has to be 'too exalted for the familiarity of names'.[45] Again, this can be understood only by referring to a notion of law, and even to a Christian sense of love as a law above the law. If love were to become a virtue definable by principles and rules then it would be no longer true to itself. Love has to fail to correspond with any description because it is the experience of the response that is not governed by any precedent or analogy. Love is 'unutterable', a 'torment', a 'delight' and a 'hunger'. As an experience, this hunger suggests that it is not self-sustaining. It is not a love of the self, but what makes the self insubstantial. To affirm love is to affirm what goes beyond the self. It is this law of love that is realised in the quotidian: ' I do not want it as a law of God, I do not want it as a human statute: let it be no sign-post to super earths and paradises'.[46]

This forceful expression has to be read very carefully. To state that it is not to be conceived on a model of either natural or positive law brings to light its peculiarity. It cannot be the law of God, as God is dead. It is not a statute, as it is not given by the state. The law has to be mandated by the self, and a personal understanding of ethical compulsion. Its good is only ever '*my*' good. In affirming this good, though, the 'my' has to be seen as the self that needs to rely on the other as enemy, as contender. If there were any sentence in Zarathustra that linked this ethic to the aesthetic of self foundation it is the preceding verse that

---

[44] Nietzsche, F., *Thus Spake Zarathustra* (Penguin, London, 1961), 87.

[45] *Ibid.*, 63.

[46] *Ibid.*, 63. For a consideration of the announcement of the new law, see Gearey, A., 'The Bible, Law and Liberation' in Freeman, M., and Lewis, A. (eds.), *Current Legal Problems* (Oxford, Oxford University Press, 1999), 263–85.

states that the self wants to 'create beyond itself'.[47] Love is the name for the creation of this law, this ethic, of over-reaching.[48]

Zarathustra is Christ as artist. Comparing Zarathustra with Christ returns to an essential problem that has always attended the writing of the law. Once the law becomes written, it is not necessarily preserved. Indeed, here we encounter a profound paradox. Writing tends both to preserve and distort the law. Religions tend to acknowledge this problem by organising themselves around a preservation of a core and licensed meaning. Heretical interpretations can then be marginalised and, if necessary, destroyed. Zarathustra can be seen as the reflex to this response. There can be no Church or lawgiver to whom one can refer to validate the meaning of the law of friendship. The individual has to give themselves the law and bear the responsibility

[47] *Ibid.*, 62.

[48] The question of friendship cannot be thought without contending with the women who appear in *Thus Spake Zarathustra*. Although Zarathustra's aphorisms appear misogynistic, they can be more properly read as suggesting that the old ways in which men and women relate to each other can no longer be sustained. For example: Zarathustra states that '[e]verything about woman is a riddle, and everything about woman has one solution: it is called pregnancy' (at 91). How can this be read? If everything about woman is a riddle, and pregnancy is the definition of woman, than this is itself a riddle rather than a statement of truth. The idea of pregnancy, on the surface, appears to be developed in fairly conventional and misogynistic terms. The hope of the woman is for the strong man, the object of her love, who will realise her desire to bear the superman. Man must fear woman; a woman must love more than she is loved. But this is a riddle. Woman, as woman, already embodies the superman, as she carries the potential to create from her own abundance. She is able to 'bear the sacrifice' that makes all other things 'valueless'. The sacrifice is the will to will oneself differently and create oneself from the solitude of one's own values. How this is to be interpreted ultimately depends on your own will to power, dear reader. The old woman, elaborating this discourse, answers the riddle with another question; woman might be the realisation that 'nothing is impossible'. The conclusion of this section retains this ambiguity: the old woman gives Zarathustra a 'truth': '[a]re you visiting women? Do not forget your whip!' To realise a friendship, to do more than simply 'visit', one would have to forget the whip and the slave tyrant complex. Men and women must overcome themselves. Zarathustra's misogyny can be read under his own doctrines as a symptom of rancour and ressentiment that occur when he is faced with a power of over-reaching and creation that appear to rival his own.

for their interpretations of the law. Coherent with this logic are those readings of Nietzsche that revel in the interpretations that his texts generate. If law as an interpretative activity has its roots in Biblical hermeneutics, then *Thus Spoke Zarathustra* is the anti-Bible. To remain true to the text is to distort it, a position that carries the caveat that the individual interpreter is always responsible for her interpretation.

Zarathustra as Christ does not announce a truth that can stand for and guarantee the meaning of a moral code or a law. In the place of the absent god can only be self-justifying and self-validating aesthetic activity. The aesthete as creator bears the burden of the creation of her own code of conduct: '[c]an you furnish yourself with your own good and evil and hang up your own will above yourself as a law? Can you be the judge and avenger of your law?'[49] A code has to take shape against an existent one. Creation is always an agonistics. The form of the announcement of this agonistic new law, then, has to echo and distort the law it attempts to supplement. The four-part division of *Thus Spake Zarathustra* recalls, in a distant way, the four Gospels. However, instead of a narrative that moves towards a conclusion that proves the truth of the story it has told, the annunciation of Christ, Zarathustra circles back towards his own beginning. Nietzsche's text both begins and ends with the address to the great star that welcomes the new day. In keeping with a 'teaching' that has to validate itself or which has to seek validation in its own repetition of the need to create anew, *Thus Spake Zarathustra* has to return the reader to the starting point of his or her reading and invite another reading. The concluding valediction to 'work' is to the initiation of an open-ended process. Like Zarathustra, the reader can 'only aspire after [his/her] work'.[50]

A similar game is being played with the repetition of *Thus spake Zarathustra*; the phrase that invariably concludes the individual 'lessons'. It is, at one level, a parody of scriptural authority.

[49] *Ibid.*, 89.
[50] *Ibid.*, 336.

Christ's words, carefully recorded by his disciples, whose accounts testify to their witness, establish a model of textual authority. Zarathustra's words have no authority other than the narrative that repeats them, and instructs the reader not to take them too seriously.

Eternal recurrence: carry that weight

Eternal recurrence is a thinking of the persistence of friendship. Recurrence should be seen as the key reformulation of the central problematic of the conjunction between aesthetics, ethics and the giving of the law. The greatest weight is the ability to will one's own law. In keeping with the contradictions of the gay science, though, this weight must be taken lightly. It must be borne in the correct spirit, as it is the 'most dangerous point of view'.[51] Holding together risk and affirmation, the weight is the 'burden' of an attitude towards time as the space of becoming in which the horizon is open to the consequences of the act. One must consider oneself equal to the greatest events of the past, the artist must write their own 'history of the everyday'.[52] There is a necessary arrogance to this ambition. Ambition is an active need to over-reach, to 'conquer', and to define oneself for oneself. Ambition or arrogance is not unqualified. There is a kind of double perspective to the history of the everyday. To see the everyday as worthy of a history, of memory and recording, is to raise it, and hence become aware of its importance. But one must not become obsessed with the minutiae of the everyday. The desirable attitude to the quotidian is the lightness of touch that is best stated simply as a turning away from what one finds distasteful: 'looking away should be [the] sole negation'.[53] If this carries with it an association of value choice, so much the better, for 'eternal recurrence' is the recurrence of this obligation to chose.

[51] Nietzsche, n. 7 *supra*, 212.
[52] *Ibid.*, 246.
[53] *Ibid.*, 223.

Reading the passages on eternal recurrence alongside those on friendship produces an intriguing set of associations. We have already seen how friendship appears in Zarathustra as an interruption in the loneliness of the soul. The dialogue of the demon that whispers the truth of eternal recurrence also occurs in 'your loneliest loneliness'.[54] It might be suggested that this interruption has something to do with impossible friendship. Eternal recurrence should not be taken as a scientific theory. The reliving of your life with 'every pain and joy . . . in the same succession and sequence' are the words of a demon. Eternal recurrence is a nightmare, a 'naked lunch' when the death of God is properly realised. There is no ultimate purpose, there is no redeemer either heavenly or secular, there is only the passage of time and your being within time. In the face of time, one has to make a choice, you can be changed or crushed. Do you fall into despair or 'have you experienced a tremendous moment'? To adopt the correct attitude to any act or any expression of will, one would have to answer the following question in the affirmative: '[d]o you desire this once more and innumerable times more?'[55] It might be easy to argue that this is bankrupt. Simply believing in an act, no matter how perverse or abhorrent, will not provide justification. The present reading glosses the words of the demon as: you have to will friendship as the only recurrent possibility of the self. Although this is arguably a responsible reading, the passage runs the risk that it will be construed differently. Eternal recurrence becomes the most dangerous moment when the freedom of the interpreter is realised by the inability of the text to constrain interpretation.

When eternal recurrence comes to be stated in *Zarathustra* it thus appears as a glyph or a riddle. Zarathustra's discourse immediately harks back to the exhortation to live dangerously in *The Gay Science*.[56] Zarathustra is addressing 'bold venturers and

[54] Nietzsche, n. 7 *supra*, 273.

[55] *Ibid.*, 274.

[56] Zarathustra's words recall the aphorism of *The Gay Science*: '[a]nd this slow spider that creeps along in the moonlight, and this moonlight itself, and I and you at this gate way . . . must we not all have been here before?', n. 36 *supra* at 179.

adventurers'[57] who are lured to the 'abyss' of infinite interpretation. The hatred of calculation recalls the language of ethical excess and sets the tone for the following allegory. A tale is told of Zarathustra's dreary progress up a mountain pass with the crippling voice of the dwarf in his head. Whether or not the dwarf is a purely symbolic figure who personifies self-doubt, or whether he is one of the characters of the book like the Kings and the Last Pope with whom Zarathustra interacts, is perhaps somewhat secondary. The key dramatic moment is the confrontation of self-doubt with the courage to believe in the affirmation of the will.

One of the keys to this attitude must be the strange conclusion to the tale. At the point when Zarathustra states the doctrine of eternal recurrence, the dwarf and the gateway marked 'now' disappear, to be replaced with another temptation. That one of the models for this riddle is the temptation of Christ is significant. If, as suggested above, Zarathustra cannot be thought without reference to the Bible, this statement of eternal recurrence seems to present itself as a kind of rethinking of the Gospel. As things are set to recur, to return, but the cost of their return is their reinterpretation, it is fitting that the doctrine of friendship should conclude with an encounter between Zarathustra and an allegorical figure of Christ. The scene shifts to a coast and a desolate moonlight. Zarathustra sees a 'young shepherd writhing' with a 'heavy, black snake' protruding from his mouth. This disturbing image brings together symbols of Christ and the devil. Zarathustra calls to the shepherd and tells him to bite the head off the snake, a cry that focuses 'all my good and evil'. After recovering, the shepherd becomes transformed in laughter. The riddle invites the following interpretation. The shepherd represents Christ whose words and teachings have become perverted, changed into their opposites. In the encounter with Zarathustra, the original animus of Christianity becomes refigured and linked with Zarathustran laughter as the free spirit that celebrates interpretative ethical energy. That

---

[57] Nietzsche, n. 36 *supra*, 176.

Zarathustra can reinterpret Christianity is the mark of his own will to power operating on an idea whose recurrence has distorted it. As an exemplary manifestation of the will to power, this restatement of Christian teaching sets a provocation to any interpreter who follows in Zarathustra's footsteps.

The aesthetic provocation to legal theory is thus to continue a will to power, to will a different way of thinking and feeling the law. If there were a summary to this chapter it would be: will the law.

4

The Province of Jurisprudence Deranged:
The Ambitions of Law and Aesthetics Scholarship

Forget Nietzsche

Any invocation of Nietzsche's name in this chapter should not be taken as a reference back to the founding father. Honest aesthetic labour must create anew and not rest on the validation of a name. As a strategy to organise this chapter, however, the idea of a gay science will be deployed as a possible grouping for a diverse collection of work that offers to carry forward the provocations of the last chapter. Under this title, writings will be encountered that have been variously described as a minor jurisprudence, queer theory, feminism, literary jurisprudence, critical race theory and a genealogy of the invisible. Running through this impossible canon are engagements with the passions and the body, with acts of self-creation, culture and style. Interacting with the law are bodies of sex, gender and race. Here forgotten histories are recovered and possible futures imagined. If there is any way of generalising across this diversity of positions, it might point to a jurisprudence that understands the existential place where law is received and reinvented.

Love and the meteor: rhetoric and the gay science.

The gay science, as a study of the chemistry of our sensations, has a concern with style, with ways of speaking and being. In the work of Peter Goodrich this becomes a question of legal rhetoric. Rhetoric is understood in the widest of senses. It is not just an analysis of textual figures as a means to creating persuasive arguments. Rhetoric is a conception of tradition as the perpetuation of certain ways of using language. To define law as rhetoric in this way would be to reaffirm the various histories of the legal institution. These traditions can be traced back to religious mythologies. In this interpretation rhetoric is a hermeneutics that transmits the past to the present. Hermeneutics derives from the name of the Greek god Hermes, whose task was to carry messages between the gods and the mortals. Rhetoric as hermeneutics is the transmission of immemorial truths that define the community that holds them dear. One can appreciate how this logic of meaning displays an essential connection between methods of interpretation in both mythology and law. Goodrich's contention is that it also underlies Christian theology, and hence feeds into the common law tradition. Modern legal interpretation can be seen as a secularisation of sacred techniques. Thus, the truths of law enshrined in the casebooks and the statutes are interpreted in a way that borrows directly from the Christian ways of reading scripture. Authority is associated with the past and its record in authoritative texts. Rhetoric is thus a 'defence of the faith', an apologia for a truth that needs to be preserved. The original meaning has to be recovered and preserved so that continuity can be established between the past and the present. Authority is established through the creation of a canon of texts. The texts themselves are carefully guarded, and licensed ways of interpretation are devised so that commentaries are built up which keep alive the essential meaning of authority. Although this form of rhetoric is central to the institution of law, it does not exhaust the possibilities that rhetoric offers.

Goodrich follows the gay science towards the promise of a different future for the sacred texts of the law. Rhetoric does not necessarily have to be connected to a recovery of the past, towards a preservation of authorities. There is within the philosophy of rhetoric an approach that celebrates the freedom of the interpreter. When the rhetorician speaks, she or he does so

in front of a particular audience with the particular objective of
persuading the hearers of the truth of the case that is being presented. Contrary to a philosophy of interpretation that argues
that meaning is always immanent to a text, preserved and ready
to pass on, rhetoric always deals with the contingent; with
scenes of argument and disputation. Its claims to truth are specific and context-based. No single gloss could exhaust a text's
meanings. As far as legal reasoning is concerned, the hazards
implicit in rhetoric can be made safe by the exclusion of certain considerations as 'irrelevant' to the case in hand. Both at
the level of individual judgements and in relation to doctrine as
a whole, the law can thus police its licensed truths. But this
cannot quite prevent the subversions of rhetoric. Unlicensed
and heretical interpretations creep into the text, especially if the
legal interpreter takes upon himself or herself the injunction to
create:

> [t]he nihilist has no confidence in the text as a transcendental value
> and meaning, the doctrinal unity of the text, far from hiding the voice
> or speech of its source, rather veils the historical and political condi-
> tions of existence as meaning. The text is here to be constituted as a
> generative and creative act of meaning.[1]

At the end of the period where the text is considered to carry a
truth, as we enter the era of the post-modern, the nihilist is the
one who accepts the need to reread the culture that has condi-
tioned him or her. This rhetoric does not return to the idea of
the text's essential truth, metaphorically the 'voice' that originally spoke it, but to the factors, cultural, historical and political, that have led to it being interpreted as presenting a doctrinal
truth. Recovering a future for the law means turning to a study
of its histories, a pursuit motivated by a genealogical spirit.

Genealogical method moves away from constructions of history that attempt to trace a coherent line of development from
the past to the present. It is critical of versions of the past that
describe the development of institutions as a working out of an
ideal scheme where past contradictions are resolved through the

---

[1] Goodrich, P., *Reading the Law* (Oxford, Blackwell, 1986), 221.

inexorable workings of history. Genealogy interprets history as a series of accidents; the present is only one of a number of radically contingent possibilities. For Goodrich the starting point of the genealogical method is the acknowledgement that the past is irretrievably absent, existing only in texts and ruins. Genealogy's concern is with the effects of this absence on the present. As a thinking of the past, genealogy can be compared to the act of memory, an act which preserves the past as a trace, an essential absence, and attempts to make this trace present in recollection. This gives both memory and genealogy a double edge. Both are a remembering and a reinvention of what has disappeared. As a study of the institution of the common law, genealogical research is committed to a refiguring of law's future. Genealogy 'looks to the plurality of institutional histories and not only to its legitimate forms',[2] forcing a rethinking of the institution in terms of what it excluded from its history, those failures or 'accidents' which suggest possible destinies that were not followed. The object of genealogy is fragmentary; it studies the margins of text, the heresies and the mistaken doctrines against which the mainstream defines itself.

The reappearance of the courts of love is linked to these concerns in Goodrich's work. Founded in Paris in 1400 by Charles VI, the courts' jurisdiction ranged over a variety of disputes from breach of the amorous confidences to violence between lovers. Organisation was non-hierarchical, the personnel chosen by a 'panel of women' to give judgments that were 'collective and poetic'.[3] Other courts with a similar jurisdiction are described in the twelfth century *Tractatus de Amore*, a work cataloguing not only a set of laws of courtly love but also the decisions of the female courts that gave judgments in these cases. The *regulae amoris* that reflect the courtly love background concern themselves with 'passion and its bodily effects'.[4] Goodrich details a number of comparisons. The courts of love replaced

[2] Goodrich, P., *Oedipus Lex* (Berkeley, Cali., University of California Press, 1995), 25.

[3] Goodrich, P., *Law in the Courts of Love* (London, Routledge, 1999).

[4] *Ibid.*, 50.

the jurisdiction of the spiritual courts, with a focus on the temporal and the material, a concern best illustrated by the words of Bernard of Clairvaux: 'we are carnal, and born of concupiscence of the flesh, so it is also necessary that our love begins with the flesh'.[5]

The *regulae amoris* constitute a code that recognises an ethical dimension to affairs of the heart. For instance, the rules state that love should end only if the lovers no longer feel a passion for each other, or if another love intervenes. In the former case the lovers are to remain bound to each other for a period of two years and to abstain from other affairs. Central to these rules is the creation of an 'ethical casuistry of relationship'.[6] This is not the rejection of the notion of regulation or the possibility of codifying human relationships, but it is a movement beyond the prescription of erotic relationships that is found in ecclesiastical law. Here is an acknowledgment that sexual relationships can be seriously considered as a matter for law, a recognition that human relationships have to be founded on an ethics of difference and the accompanying recognition of the importance of the fleshy body as much as the soul.

Goodrich's work has gathered many supporters and detractors. Some castigated what appeared to be a turn from political engagement to historical obfuscation, others a modish flirting with continental philosophy at the expense of analytical rigour. The only question that can be addressed here, though, is the extent to which it realises an aesthetic jurisprudence, a gay science, and a joyous recreation of value. Goodrich acknowledges that law's hold is maintained because it reproduces itself at a doctrinal level through a pedagogy that passes on its institutional forms in a quiescent way.[7] For critical work to make sense it must propose different ways of thinking, reading and living the law. Love seems simultaneously to make demands excessive of legal form and yet, with the discovery of the Courts of Love, to require a kind of regulation that returns to the law. Does this

[5] *Ibid.*

[6] *Ibid.*, 52.

[7] Goodrich, n. 1 *supra*, 210.

commitment to the law betray any truly radical ideas? Does the critics' love of the law invalidate his criticism? Can Goodrich will a new law?[8] These questions must be suspended as Goodrich's project is still ongoing, but as an exercise in creative provocation it has to be recognised as taking seriously the need to reinvent Critical Legal Studies as an aesthetics of law. It can be furthered by locating those fellow travellers who examine modes of legal belonging and the tensions that arise within them.

Black Orpheus

Critical Race Theory places on the agenda a kind of thinking that can examine the dynamics of the legal institution. Its creativity is the ability to find in the old the beginnings of the new.[9] These elements can best be appreciated in a study of the following extract from the work of Anthony Farley. It is part of a wider argument that looks at the law's perpetuation of cultural patterns of racism[10] at the level of the body itself, a body that is essential to the experiences of one's own personhood. Like Nietzsche, this writing courts misunderstanding. Its hostility to the 'we shall overcome' mentality of the civil liberties movement occasionally reads like Nietzsche's own attacks on morality. It is, however, necessary to be critical to the original movement to carry its legacy forward.

The following extract begins with a reflection on the kind of experience that may seem irrelevant to the law. The writer is recounting an experience of watching a Tarzan movie. In the movie, the white hunters are toiling up a steep mountain pass. Suddenly, one of the nameless black porters slips and plunges

---

[8] Goodrich's 'The Critics Love of the Law' (1999) *Law and Critique* 343–60 can be read as containing elements of autocritique in posing this very question.

[9] This is not just to repeat the received wisdom that it is now Critical Race Theory that carries forward the energy of Critical Legal Studies, this is a kind of thinking that can transmute base materials into the possibility of new forms. It is critical, self-reflective and affirms its own creation.

[10] For a exploration of these ideas see Fitzpatrick, P., *The Mythology of Modern Law* (London, Routledge, 1992).

over the precipice. The reaction of the party is to exclaim: 'the supplies!' Should this seem irrelevant, it is connected to the following more extended narrative. It is a story of a school trip 'on a spring day of my eighth grade year, 1976'.[11] The reader is immediately aware of a personal recollection, of a time and a place, a year and a season that are part of an ongoing life. It is a homely scene, set on a 'bus chartered for a class trip to Washington D.C.'. There is a sense of community, of belonging. This also operates at an allegorical level. The bus is taking the children to the nation's capital, the site of the law-making body and a symbol of what holds the nation together. Farley is describing a 'schoolmate' combing her 'long, brown hair', someone 'tall and cool and pretty'. There is a sense both of admiration and drama in her combing her hair 'slowly and deliberately'. She knows that her schoolmates are watching her and appreciating her body and the narrative subtly enacts the gaze that passes between the children and the girl, and is acknowledged by her in her slow, deliberate actions. She then turns and, addressing the group, asks whose comb she has been using; 'one of our classmates answered in a mirthful voice: '[i]t's Farley's comb'. The author records his response: ' I, Farley, was the only black person on this otherwise all-white school trip to the nation's capital'. As the bus breaks into laughter, '[t]he girl with the long brown hair turned crimson and began to cry in loud, long sobs. The sobs quickly turned into the sounds of retching which were accompanied by shudders running through her hunched form. She may have vomited'. Whilst 'her personal trauma unfolded, accompanied by squeals of laughter . . . I said nothing'.

The image of vomiting that concludes the story is part of a wider metaphoric chain.[12] It presents an extreme bodily reaction as a figure of a more or less explicit social attitude of whites to blacks. They have to be removed, vomited out of the social body. Setting the scene on a bus also connects it with the quintessential

[11] Farley, A., 'The Black Body as Fetish Object' (1997) *Oregon Law Review* 480.
[12] See also Farley, A., 'Thirteeen Stories' (1999) *Tuoro Law Review* 2.

civil rights image of the 'segregated bus of the 1950's'.[13] The point is that racism remains in different but no less powerful forms. Most importantly, though, the act of recording and writing about this experience manifests a kind of thought, a way of appropriating experience; a means, ultimately, of finding in the body a site of resistance. A tension is created between the silence of the character in the story and the fact that he is now writing the story, giving a voice to his previous silence. The character 'Farley' becomes an object for the author Farley as part of the definition of self with which this story is concerned. He draws the conclusion: '[a]ll of us experienced our connection through the colorline as a physical sensation, not as an abstract idea'.[14] Racism is a sensuous reality. What unites the children on the bus is a complicity in the 'microaggressions' of racism. This is experienced at the level of the body, its reactions of nausea, shame and self-loathing. Community is organised around the ridicule and exclusion of the 'other'. Race is understood as a 'sadomasochistic form of pleasure'.[15]

The description of racism as 'ideology made flesh' suggests an application of the gay science. Furthermore, Farley affirms that understanding racism would require a genealogy that discovers its enabling conditions.[16] This remains presupposed by the idea that whiteness and blackness are constructed. 'Whiteness' has to be 'created' in the same way that the social world as a whole is constructed. The creation of whiteness is predicated on the fetishisation of the black body. The white body is experienced as pleasure and the black body is denigrated as loathsome and ugly. Farley argues that the extent of the 'colourline' can be further studied in the masochistic attitude of blacks towards their own bodies. This 'poetics of location'[17] bears all the marks of the thinking of an underground man: '[c]ivil rights will not create the

---

[13] *Tuoro Law Review* 2., 492.

[14] *Ibid.*, at 480.

[15] *Ibid.*, at 461.

[16] See Fitzpatrick, n. 10 *supra*.

[17] Farley, n. 12 *supra*, 486.

raceless society. We reify the colorline even as we attempt to draft
statutes to eliminate it from our lives—this is because we continue
to preserve the notion of race'.[18] In accepting your body as
defined through race, there is an act of identification, of self-creation, that could have been otherwise. To become aware that you
are a 'fetish object' is to become a 'subject': '[w]e are condemned,
not to slavery, but to freedom'.[19] Sartrean echoes in this statement indicate a thinking that, to summarise brutally, connects the
personal and the political.[20] Within the wider complex of this
article, it might also return to the sense in which this thought is
also an engagement with solidarity. Writing does not isolate the
thinker. To 'refound' thought there is an obligation to move away
from what is 'outlived and decayed', whilst acknowledging that
what remains in the decayed form is the spark of a force that once
had a foundational energy. This is consistent with the notion that
the underground man can both perceive the hold of the new
form, and through his own artistry and researches 'sublimate'[21]
the force that has grown old and rigid into new forms. If this
appears 'absurd'[22] it is because one has to contend with the arrogance of any thinker who believes that she can contend with the
forces of tradition, that can offer any reinvented forms.

[18] *Ibid.*, at 528.

[19] *Ibid.*, at 530.

[20] On the problem of Sartre's influence on Critical Legal Studies , see Schlag
P., 'The Problem of the Subject' (1991) *Texas Law Review* 7. Schlag argues that
it is the 'separation' between subject and object, between 'consciousness and social
roles' (at 1690) that allows Critical Legal Studies to make the arguments that it
does. This 'problematic and relentles0sly recursive subject-object hierarchy' (at
1685) is not a feature of the social world, but a product of a particular description of the social world. Farley reads Sartre in such a way that this critique is dis-
armed. He uses Sartre to reveal the operating assumptions in a particular
description of the social world that utilises a specifically racist version of the subject–object hierarchy. An interesting encounter could be staged between the aesthetics of Farley's work, and Schlag's more extended consideration of the aesthetic
in *The Enchantment of Reason* (Duke University Press, Durham N.C. 1998).

[21] Nietzsche, F., *Daybreak* (Cambridge, Cambridge University Press, 1982), 5.
[22] Ibid., 3.

How queer

The law operates at the level of the body. It articulates and organises desire. Desire does not exist in some rarefied form, but always belongs to bodies with their particular desires. Feminist scholarship has, of course, discussed the ways in which the law has constructed the female body. The concern here, though, is in some ways an extension and in other ways a break with more conventional feminism. The question is that of the law's construction of same-sex desire. We could indeed speak of a genital order.[23] It is difficult, if not against the spirit of this kind of scholarship, to label it 'queer theory'. A claim that there is one overarching theoretical position might even be a severe distortion. The category 'queer' may simply operate to deny the real differences that exist between those who are 'queer theorists'. Indeed, the very term 'queer' has to be understood as suggesting the disturbance, rather than the settling of notions of foundational identity.[24] With this in mind, the work of Les Moran will be considered as an exemplification of queer theory as gay science. It returns to the problematic, inescapable tensions that exist in the relations between lovers, strangers and friends.[25]

Moran's work is built on the essential insight that law operates through a classification of our pleasures, a process that can perhaps be glimpsed most clearly through those categories that are considered pathological. This can be understood as an investigation of the categorising of values to create the legal and the illegal, the normal and the abnormal. Once categories are created

---

[23] Moran, L., *The Homosexual(ity) of Law* (London, Routledge, 1996), 167.

[24] See Davies, M., 'Taking the Inside Out; Sex and Gender in the Legal Subject' in Naffine, N., and Owens, J.O. (eds.), *Sexing the Subject of Law* (London, Sweet and Maxwell, 1997), 26–46 and Davies, M., 'Feminist Appropriations: Law, Property and Personality' (1994) 3 *Social and Legal Studies* 365.

[25] See Rich, A., in Moran, L., Monk, D., and Beresford, S. (eds.), *Legal Queeries, Lesbian, Gay and Transgender Legal Studies* (London, Cassell, 1998), 24.

they can in turn be described in moral terms and entire ways of being either criminalised and hence in need of punishment, medicalisation, cure or rehabilitation. Law has a lexicon that it can use to define the behaviour it observes and give it meaning. Rather than being invisible to the law, acts considered to be homosexual have a vast body of description. This is not to say that crimes such as buggery and sodomy have always had the same meaning. What are important are the taxonomies, the techniques and practices that allow 'crimes' to be given a meaning.

Consider the following way in which the male body appears at the level of the official record. In one recorded case, the agents of law enforcement recorded a certain Horton's passage through the West End of London. Horton is recorded as walking in a rough circle, from lavatory to lavatory, returning to his starting point in Leiceseter Square. Although Horton spoke to no-one, he occasionally smiled at other men. On his arrest he was found to be wearing make up. His reply to the arresting officer was 'oh dear this is very annoying'.[26] In this case there was no evidence of a complaint. Other than the eyes of the law, there were no witnesses. Without this surveillance Horton would just have been another anonymous man. He is turned into an object to be classified and punished. Acts that were ambiguous or had no special meaning for the individual concerned are given official meaning. The language of the police report becomes that of the judgment of Lord Alverstone. Horton's reply to the arresting officer and his demeanour become constituted as evidence of soliciting, even though there is no other evidence. The law constitutes Horton as a homosexual. Within the texts of the law homosexual desire is thus encoded in a certain way.

But the public record is already a kind of abstraction, a form of misrepresentation.

The science of surveillance in this exemplary case has to extract and fix certain meanings from a social performance that is inherently complex. One has to grasp the erotic possibilities offered by a public convenience. These possibilities operate in a context

---

[26] Moran, n. 23 *supra*, 136.

where acts that are considered private are performed publicly. Taboos that surround both defecation and urination mean that a lavatory is encoded in a particular way. People are separated; privacy is maintained. These features also offer themselves to those who want to engage in sexual acts, but want to maintain a certain privacy. The potentials offered by this kind of space for a kind of sexual activity thus feed into the law. The Sexual Offences Act of 1967 speaks this language of acceptable and unacceptable acts by using a distinction between legitimate and illegitimate private acts in public spaces. Furthermore, this Act authorises a kind of legitimate and authoritative public speech about these acts. But there is also a counter-discourse, a different way of talking about and giving these experiences meaning. Rather than seeing them as acts to be criminalised, they could be considered a kind of performance, a playing out of roles, an expression of a form of sexuality that is neither coercive nor committal.[27]

However, these alternative ways of speaking and behaving are not themselves uncontaminated by the discourse of stigma and control. Indeed, the very existence of subcodes allows for their exploitation by policemen who have to mimic the sartorial and behavioural styles to apprehended homosexuals. It comes down to a question of becoming responsible for a particular set of representations, particular acts of desire. The law prohibits and regulates homosexual desire just as it does heterosexual desire. However, within this regime of regulation, homosexual desire is encoded in a different way and iniquities are set up. Does this mean that queer studies make for a reformist strategy, where the law can ultimately legitimise queer identities? The problem with this interpretation is that it might underestimate the extent to which dissent can be included in the system and made safe.[28] A way forward might be a kind of 'cultural calumny'.[29]

[27] Moran, n. 23 *supra*, 149.

[28] Becker L.C., 'Queering Theory: An Essay on the Conceit of Revolution in Law' in Moran, Monk and Beresford, n. 25 *supra*.

[29] As a strategy this makes use of a reclamation of the Judaeo-Christian narratives of struggle without end that returns to a kind of Nietzschean reappropriation of the norm to create the 'counter norm'. See Becker, n. 25 *supra*, 188.

Scholarship may have an obligation to argue for reform of the law, but it must also acknowledge that there can be no escape from a regime of representation. Queer theory must pose the question of who controls representations of normal and abnormal behaviour, and hence the fate of bodies and desire.[30]

Queer theory thus provokes a question of style in the same way that the work on rhetoric raised this essential category.

The passion of reading

What remains interesting about the politics of reading developed in queer theory is the notion that an act of interpretation is always specific to a reader, to a horizon and to a set of experiences of the world. Interpretation and the texts to be interpreted gain their importance and significance from this experience. Canons are less important than the concerns of the interpreter, the individual talent. From this perspective, law and literature scholarship becomes a search for an active creation of value. Maria Aristodemou's work is an exemplification of this process. Behind acts of reading are always questions of passion and desire. What is also distinctive of this work is its focus on the figure of the maternal body, the great aporia of Nietzschean ethics.

---

[30] See Loizidou, E., 'Intimate Queer Celluloid: Heavenly Creatures and Criminal Law', in Moran, Monk and Beresford, n. 25 *supra*, 167–85. Queer theory takes the image seriously. This is perhaps why it has exerted a significant influence on the study of the intersection between film and law. Loizidou's study of *Heavenly Creatures*, a film directed by Peter Jackson, is exemplary not just for its discussion of the medium, but also for its implicit Nietzschean poetics of the self. The film concerns the erotic relationship between two girls, Pauline and Juliet. Pauline's mother objects to her daughter's passion, but so intense is Pauline's devotion to Juliet that they choose to murder her in an attempt to stay together. They are tried, convicted and sentenced to life imprisonment. Concluding the film is a sentence: 'it was a condition of their release that they never meet again'. Loizidou argues that *Heavenly Creatures* can be read as a way of understanding the criminal law that is not predicated on traditional legal sources. The film disturbs the extent to which the law's general categories can locate all individuals. If one privileges this operation of the law, one misses the extent to which law constructs the bodies that it then sentences. The film can show both the symbolic of law, and what disturbs that symbolic order.

Aristodemou's work is founded on a critique of how conventional law and literature scholarship has created a field of study. Traditionally, law and literature scholars have been content to work with models of literature that see it primarily as the product of particularly gifted authors who communicate their insights to the readers of their work. In contradiction to this view, it can be argued that the literary text needs to be placed in the context of its reception. For instance, Aristodemou's reading of Shakespeare rests on an assumption that the play is read differently at different times and in different contexts. This is not just to do with the death of the author[31] or with the argument that a text is essentially open to interpretation and resists the closure of one essential meaning. Rather, the text becomes a mirror to the self. The reader brings to the text certain anxieties and concerns of her own operating at conscious and unconscious levels: 'every reader comes to literature with dirty hands'.[32]

The responsiveness of a text to these concerns, the way in which it seems to have already inscribed them in its own narrative or symbolic economy, can become a way of distinguishing texts that are worthy of attention. To some extent, the worth of a text reflects a kind of writing, an 'excessiveness' that means that no one reading will exhaust the resources of the text.[33] Furthermore, it means that literature is more than simply an 'unmediated' mimetic account of the world. If this were the case, once criticism had discovered the truth of its representations, the text would become inert and no longer able to fascinate the reader with its mysteriousness. Aristodemou's work attempts to steer between a surrender to the strangeness of the literary, and the reductionism that sees the literary as merely an object to be interpreted. Her starting point is that the reader is already seduced by a text; desire is caught up with what one reads, and how one chooses to read. Literature, it could be said, is involved with the production of subjectivity.

[31] Aristodemou, M., 'Law and Desire in Measure for Measure' (1998) *Law and Critique* 117–40, at 117.

[32] *Ibid.*, 118.

[33] This is very close to the Shelleyan idea of poetry.

These matters are explored in Aristodemou's reading of Toni Morrison's *Beloved*. *Beloved* tells the story of a woman called Sethe, her daughter Denver and the ghost of Sethe's daughter who gives the book its name.[34] The book is concerned with memories of slavery, and with the case of the slave Margaret Garner who murdered her own child. In arguing that she should have been tried for murder, rather than theft, the abolitionists sought to use the courts to draw attention to the denigration of the person in slavery. *Beloved* is an attempt to recover the memories and stories of women like Margaret Garner whose voices are absent from the records of the authorities and also tend not to appear in the alternative 'up from slavery narratives'. *Beloved* is thus representative of a kind of theoretical practice that Aristodemou recommends for law and literature scholarship. Like Morrison's novel, scholarship should look to these different voices, memories and knowledges. This kind of writing demands a different kind of reading. *Beloved* is composed in such a way as to have neither beginning, middle nor end. It does not have an 'omniscient narrator'[35] who might offer a coherent shape to the overall book. Instead it consists of a number of narrative lines that are associated with the various characters in the book. The reader has to 'participate as a co-author of the text'.[36] Its model is thus more of an oral tradition that accepts that there can be no definitive story. The story can be changed by anyone who chooses to tell it. This essential plurality of form was also central to the images of community and self that the stories define; as Aristodemou writes: 'the employment of competing voices reminds us further that self recognition can only take place in dialogue with others, a dialogue that leaves us conscious that we are "one and the other at the same time"'.[37]

It is this question, as it interfaces with the question of infanticide, that makes *Beloved* the site of a difficult, aporetic ethics.

[34] Aristodemou, M., 32 *New Formations* (1997), 40.
[35] *Ibid.*, 41.
[36] *Ibid.*
[37] *Ibid.*, 43.

The pregnant mother is both herself and other to herself. In this sense she is of no category. Motherhood may be impossible to define, to set neatly within the language that separates self and other. This is not, though, necessarily, an essentialism. Mother and child are a particularly acute embodiment of the paradox that the other may be the person closest to us. In the thought of the French philosopher Emmanuel Levinas, this takes the name 'proximity' and provides the provocation for an original ethics where the other provides the self with the very possibility of its subjectivity. In Morrsion's text, this ethic is dramatised so that the once silenced 'slave mother' becomes an ethical subject who has to make a profoundly difficult decision. Sethe's narrative presents her as split, able to murder the child she loves to prevent her falling into the hands of the slave owner; an act that, as Morrison herself explained, although the right thing to do, Sethe had no right to do. The logic of the law could not understand such a decision. But 'Sethe's murder of Beloved takes place out of a love that is not guided by rationality but is singular, unique and unrepeatable'.[38] Although based on this intense love, Sethe is not exonerated, neither is she judged. This paradox has to be preserved as an authentic ethics.

As this concern with the mother and child might suggest, the privileged moment for a consideration of the construction of subjectivity is the body itself. In an engagement with Angela Carter's fairy tales, Aristodemou discovers an important figuring of women as lawmakers. This turn to Carter is interesting in itself, as her work remains outside the traditional canon of law and literature because it tends to reinterpret the 'frivolous' forms of the fairy tale that remains distinct from the 'serious' tradition of the American and the European novel. Carter's re-workings of the fairy tale, though, are an attempt to imagine different relationships between men and women. What would happen, for instance, if Beauty refused to marry the Beast? This twist in the traditional story raises large questions for the discourse of law. As Aristodemou points out, the idea of marriage, the exchange

[38] *New Formations*, 46.

of women as the foundation of legitimacy and genealogy is central to law's creation of a world where women are merely objects to seal alliances between men. For Beauty not to marry the Beast, though, is not a straightforward refusal of any relationship between women and men. Re-imagining the ending of the story can be read as suggesting that women and men need to relate to each other differently and this difference is an alternative foundation for notions of legitimacy. This would force a consideration of love, but outside its constructions of the patriarchal tradition. Feminists have drawn attention to a belief and practice of love as indirection, and this is now expressly connected to a female imagination of the law. This law of love would 'reach out to the other as subject rather than assimilating him/her as object'.[39] Even if this is dismissed as a utopian fantasy, it is a provocation for a different imagination and a creation of alternative forms.

What comes out of this work, then, is the focus on the construction of self. There can be no guarantee that literature will save us, or save the law. What it can do is to place a critical focus on the way in which we become people. This is a subject for study by a gay science of law whose interest in the construction of the social is to recover a creativity that maintains that the creative soul can always begin again.

Begin again.

Antigone's destiny: the ancient condition of modern law

Costas Douzinas' reading of Antigone appropriates for an aesthetic jurisprudence one of the main texts of the western tradition. That the play has already been read jurisprudentially means that the stakes are high. It was the touchstone of one of the most important reflections on the nature of the state and law by the German philosopher G. W. F. Hegel. Could it be that

[39] Aristodemou, M., 'Fantasies of Women as Lawmakers: Empowerment or Entrapment in Angela Carter's Bloody Chambers' in Freeman, M., and Lewis, A., (eds.), *Law and Literature: Current Legal Issues* (Oxford, OUP, 1999) 213.

this text concerns a way of understanding the law and opposition to the law that Hegel did not articulate?[40] The concluding section of this chapter will interrogate Douzinas' reading of this provocative text.

The tragic action of the play focuses on Antigone's denial of the law of the state as exemplified in the command of King Creon, who has forbidden the burial of her brother, the traitor Polynices.[41] Antigone claims that her refusal to obey the law of the state is justified by her obedience to a more profound law, the divine law, which obligates her to the care of Polynices' corpse. As a punishment, she is entombed alive. Creon's arrogance also leads to a tragic conclusion; his own death and the fall of the state.

Hegel understood the play as illustrating a number of essential conflicts between nature, culture, the individual and the community. The play is presented as a series of contrasts. Creon speaks for positive law that has to be universally applied and is directed towards the preservation of the state. He is rational, objective and inflexible. Antigone, on the other hand, is under the obligation of divine law. Her passionate attachment to her brother is not the kind of act that can be universalised. It is private, located in the family, and blood intimacy rather than public and rational. These contrasts are generalised out. Antigone represents a female nature that is intuitive, ethical in a private sense and orientated to the family and individuals. Creon, and human law, are on the side of culture. Personal and subjective attachments are dissolved in the objectivity of the state. For Hegel, these opposites can be resolved only if the family is directed towards the preservation of the state. Rather than being focused on itself, the family must find its meaning in supporting the greater good of the community.

---

[40] Chanter, T., *The Ethics of Eros* (London, Routledge, 1995), 80. 'It is very important to question again the foundations of the symbolic order in mythology and tragedy, because they deal with a landscape which installs itself in the imagination and then, all of a sudden, becomes law'.

[41] Douzinas, C., and Warrington, R., *Justice Miscarried* (Hemel Hempstead, Harvester, 1994).

This reading of the fate of the law is resisted. *Antigone* cannot be understood as a celebration of the law of the state. It is the impossible articulation of a mystery as ancient as it is modern, a problem at the root of any ethical order, the 'wild irrational force of the must'.[42] Consider the following dialogue:

> Ismene: You cannot mean . . . to bury him? Against the order?
> Antigone: Yes! He is my brother . . . I must bury him myself . . .
> Ismene: Then go if you must wild, irrational as you are.[43]

What is the force of the 'must'? It is, of course, Antigone's passionate refusal to obey Creon's order. At another level, the 'must' could be taken as a metaphor for the compulsion to stand against a law that appears unjust. Any proper understanding of the 'must' means placing it within the context of the play.

The mythology underlying *Antigone* stages in particularly dramatic terms what could be called the law of self-creation. *The Ode to Man* links the deity called Moirai to the nature of the human being. Fate or destiny has determined that Man, of all the animals, should develop reason and the terrible powers that come with this faculty. Although Man has reason he is still subject to the wider jurisdiction of fate. Moirai, as a plural noun, suggests that fate is not a single 'overarching' concept. If fate is 'always plural'[44] it is not pure determinism, but holds open a possibility of human action. It is this tension that informs the action of Greek drama, where the tragic hero's fate is partially determined but still open to the choices that the character makes. Consider Oedipus. He is both the victim of forces outside his control that compel him to murder his father and marry his mother but he is also able to determine his own destiny in that he chooses to blind himself and become a wanderer. When the tragic hero trusts his fate to destiny he does so for grounds that are opaque in the moment of decision. After events have played themselves out, reflecting on the decision allows a retrospective interpretation that may or may not account for the 'meaning' of the hero's fate.

---

[42] *Ibid.*, 26.
[43] *Ibid.*
[44] *Ibid.*

Destiny as Moirai underlies *Antigone* and moves towards a dramatisation of the 'must' of law. Privileging the idea of destiny determines more clearly a possible ground of responsibility: 'we acquire our freedom and singularity in desiring feverently and unto death this unknown law of destiny'.[45] This is the crucial moment when a person accepts his or her fate and gives it a meaning. The subject is both 'author' and 'victim'. For Antigone it is the moment that she chooses to bury Polynices and thus seal her fate. Antigone herself does not *know* why she acts other than in responding to a particular situation, a moment when she finds herself before her brother's corpse and thus accepts the blind hand that destiny has dealt her. But there is one vital factor that has not been considered so far: eros.

When Antigone comes to explain her own actions, she states 'I was born to love, not to hate',[46] indicating a level of desire that, given her acceptance of her fate, is inseparable from *thanatos*, her death drive. In plumbing Antigone's desire, there is thus a return to previous concerns with death as an existential possibility, 'its recognition and acceptance'[47] individuates. Death is the '*differentia specifica*'. But what does it mean to say that Antigone is in love with her own death? As Douzinas stresses, this is not Platonic eros that makes for balance and harmony, nor the love of the Hegelian odyssey that transcends the differences of the parents in the child. Eros is the destructive force evoked by poetess Sappho as the whirlwind off the mountains. *Antigone* thus raises the same questions that psychoanalysis attempts to answer. Looked at through Lacanian lenses, Antigone's love is the answer to the question posed by the other. Not only does Antigone's eros give her life its ultimate meaning, it 'fills' the hole in the other which would otherwise remain a crushing absence. In classic Lacanian terms, Antigone is ethical because she does not give way on her desire. This makes her dangerous. She rejects the law of the state in answering, in the only way that she can, the demand of her desire.

45 Chanter, T., *The Ethics of Eros* (London, Routledge, 1995), 74.
46 *Ibid.*, 75.
47 *Ibid.*, 76.

In the moment that she rejects the law, Antigone acts not so much from an ethical idea, but from a 'somatic encounter' with the physicality of her brother. The 'must' in other words can be traced to an encounter between people. In turn, this presupposes that Antigone is a specific individual, that her action and her fate are irretrievably *hers*:

> The ontology of alterity . . . is based on the absolute proximity of the most alien. When the self comes to constitute itself, before it faces the I, it must face the I's relationship with the other. Subjectivity is constituted through this opening.[48]

The subject is created in its relationship with the other. At the risk of generalising, Antigone's experience can provide a glyph to understand the diverse moments of the wisdom of the inessential considered above. In its various ways, it finds arguments for action, for mandating new values in the commitment to projects in the world. Whether these express themselves in terms of the new forms of law, or new values that escape the categories of the law, they emerge from encounters with the material circumstances of life.

To misquote Ezra Pound, all mythologies tell us something about ourselves. What does Douzinas' mythology suggest about the law, and our relationship to the law? This chapter concludes with a reading of *Antigone* because it displays what is at stake in the various projects that this chapter has examined. It is necessary to contend with the past, with the way law constructs itself, in order to face the future. This reading of *Antigone* figures a return to one of the sources of the western tradition as a broader attempt to imagine a different future for the law. But why should one want to return? It could be said that the return is always a dangerous and double moment. Psychoanalysis describes the return as trauma. Our return is always a reliving of an original wound that will always be with us. Even if you can return, at best you will know that you are wounded and must always be so to be a social being. If you cannot work through your symptoms,

---

[48] *Ibid.*

you are, at worst, condemned to repeat them without even the knowledge of how they condition you. This is a concern that Douzinas' work has at its heart. However, the return is a necessary redemptive act, 'involved in the duplicity of a backward look that is firmly established in the politics of the future'.[49] How does this offer a different understanding of the return? It might testify to the control of the past over the present. Our fate may be only ever to repeat the traumas that we cannot face. In this sense Antigone's act becomes interpreted as a kind of terrorism that repeats the violence of the state it opposes. But perhaps it is more properly a question of the spirit and the will that informs the way in which we make the past anew in the present. From this perspective, *Antigone* becomes a counter of a different possibility.[50] Douzinas' reading suggests that there is always a potential in the law for its re-figuring, for its ethical reinvention. It is not the case that we are limited by a single fantasmatic version of the law or social being. Although it would be to commit an act of historical bad faith to return to the violent fantasies of opposition, it would also be a surrender to fail to engage with a kind of utopian imagination. Violence can be willed as a kind of rhetoric, a symbolic violence of argument that can locate in the law those moments when it can be opened to ethics.

How can the ambitions of law and aesthetics scholarship be sustained?

---

[49] See Douzinas C., *The End of Human Rights; Critical Thought at the Turn of the Century* (Oxford, Hart Publishing, 2000), 376.

[50] See also Ari Hirvonen's reading of Hamlet in Hirvonen, A. (ed.), *Polycentricity* (London, Pluto Press, 1998), 192–239.

5
Interruptions

An aesthetics of law has to bring together theory and practice in staging interventions in legal discourse. Providing a starting point will be a critical reading of the work of Roberto Unger, whose recent work *Politics*, more than any other recent manifestation of American Critical Legal Studies, has a vision of aesthetic 'negative capability' at its core. Negative capability emerges as the most recent development of a perennial concern, the capacity to reinvent our emotional connection with others outside institutional structures that are meant to contain and condition them. However, *Politics* is only partially successful in realising these ends. It will be necessary to follow lines of fracture, to provide an internal critique of *Politics* that divorces the concept of institutional imagination from the specifics of the reforms envisioned and some of its theoretical underpinnings. Rather than a vision of law completely transformed, a legal aesthetics could be reinterpreted as an interruption of the dialogue that the institution holds with itself. Completing the chapter will be a discussion of a line of cases that saw the birth and death of the family assets doctrine. The analysis will concern the extent to which the law can be interrupted and revised social relationships encouraged.

Unger's alembic

To return to some of the themes developed earlier, *Politics* can be approached as a response to reification, an attempt to think through the troubled, romantic distinction between law and life.[1]

[1] These terms still have a currency of sorts in recent American critical jurisprudence. See, for example, Balkin, J., 'Transcendental Deconstruction,

Appreciating this means referring to a companion text, *Passion*, that reads as the latest bulletin in a project to create a theory of lived experience. A brief review of the salient features of this vision will focus on the question whether it represents a useful contribution to a legal aesthetics.

Borrowing from both Christian theology and modernist social theory, *Passion* affirms that the self cannot be conceived as the centre of the world[2] as it must exist alongside others. Just as others can appear to overwhelm the self, the self can make 'disproportionate' demands on the other. The tension between these two imperatives is the central problematic of social life. Individuals have to live in circumstances of mutual trust, to allow people to 'imagine themselves connected in untried ways to other people'.[3] Love is the developed sense of this joy of connection. There is no real separation between the intimate experience of love and love amongst friends, or even a wider group of people, even though these later relationships tend to be described in terms of sympathy or solidarity.[4] In its most realised form, love involves a self-reflection that has to pass through a realisation of death as the mark of both separation and dependency on others. This is the ultimate challenge to self-identity; the shattering of a 'frame of reference' that takes itself

Transcendent Justice' (1994) 92 *Michigan Law Review* 1131–83. One can see that the disruptive influence of life is at the heart of Jack Balkin's version of deconstruction. Life is the distinction, the 'gap', between the forms of justice and their problematic articulation. Balkin's notion of transcendental justice is understood not as a search for ideals that exist outside the society that conditions them but by an acknowledgement that to be human is to be marked by a need to evaluate, 'to value'. This forces a realisation that we have to construct an idea of justice in the world of culture. There is a difference: the articulation of values in culture is different from the values themselves. This is the 'gap' that deconstruction addresses. 'Transcendental deconstruction' is an acknowledgement of the 'human capacity for judgement' which goes beyond the 'positive norms' of culture. At the same time, these transcendental values are 'inchoate', they are articulated in culture. Legal theory has to navigate this tension between law and value.

[2] Unger R., *Passion* (New York, Free Press, 1984), 4.

[3] *Ibid.*, 74.

[4] *Ibid.*, 222.

as fixed and absolute. It prompts an insight into contingency, and the hope that something might survive the ravages of personal extinction.

It is the need to respond to experience, to its surprises and risks, and to alter the sense of self in the face of these encounters, that allows the reflexivity of the love relationship. There can be no illusions. This view of the world can lead to disillusionment, or even revert to the mere acceptance of life as dull routine: 'inherent in social life is the danger that all forms of exchange and community will be used to entrench the exercise of ongoing, unaccountable, and unreciprocated power'.[5] If love is an experience of coming to the self through a passionate relationship with someone who is other to the self, the refusal to return affection can be fatal. In the 'darkness' of the world of others, this is frequently the sad truth. Precisely because love is so rare, there is a need to suspend disbelief about its possibility without succumbing to despair. Love can be supplemented by 'sympathy and fellow feeling',[6] recognition of the despair of the other.

What are we to make of Unger's history of the self? Can the notion of a social love be redeemed from Christian social theory for the benefit of cynical post-modernity? Like the gay science, Unger's text is self-consciously joyous,[7] a development of gay wisdom within the dour world of social theory. Indeed, Zarathustra's enemy, without whom the self could not appear, also recurs in the location of the self as the social self who desires to be accepted 'by one another and to become, through this acceptance, freer to reinvent ourselves'.[8] To what extent, though, does it realise the experimental, heretical energies that have been associated with this way of thinking? Even to begin a social theory of law with such a concept is perhaps an advance on those accounts that conceive of human association as inherently pathological and in immediate need of the law. From

[5] *Ibid.*, 96.
[6] *Ibid.*, 224.
[7] *Ibid.*, 72.
[8] *Ibid.*, vii.

a theological perspective, it would be interesting to ask whether Unger has sufficiently dispensed with a pessimistic strain that always accompanied the more liberatory aspects of Christian belief.[9] These questions must, however, largely remain outside the scope of this book. This late in the day, it would be foolish to enter into an argument about the ultimate truth of these claims, but at least within the world of legal theory, a counter-myth of human nature is welcome. Furthermore, in more contemporary terms, *Passion* reverses the traditional privilege of liberal legal theory on the importance of the individual, and endeavours to think in terms of solidarity. But the book never reads as a trashing of the liberal tradition. It is offered as a historic compromise, a theory that resists degenerating into either a re-hashed critique of liberalism or a rejection of a communism that champions a resistance to a repressive social order. Whilst these considerations are important for a location of Unger's recent work within contemporary legal thought, the pressing issue for this chapter is a little more limited. To what extent is this theory of love useful for an aesthetics of law?

Passion does, first of all, beg the question whether the careful, tentative work that constituted Nietzsche's own studies is best realised in this account of a Christian ethics. Unger's work may ultimately have to be judged against the other great attempts to define genealogies of the ethics and the passions, which remain ongoing and consciously open-ended to a far greater degree. Related to this problem is a cast of thought that deals in great, sweeping, historical conceptions. To the extent that this interfaces with the need to think of law totally transformed, it will be held in a certain amount of suspicion. A more substantive concern, though, is the issue of whether legal aesthetics needs to link itself to a theory of love. Although the work reviewed in the previous chapter certainly seems to subscribe to an ethic of solidarity, can this be synthesised with the idea of love? There are certainly problems. For instance, Douzinas' evocation of eros appears

---

[9] See Gearey, A., 'Rereading St. Augustine' in Tadros, V., Douglas–Scott, S., Oliver, P., (eds.), *Faith in Law* (Oxford, Hart Publishing, 1999), 53–67.

more pagan than Unger's reliance on a Christian tradition[10] and
the absence of any sustained consideration of feminist work or
same-sex desire means that *Passion* is limited, if not flawed. Any
final resolution of this problem is outside the scope of this short
book. However, to the extent that *Passion* can be co-ordinated
with the concerns discussed in the previous chapter, a strategic
alliance could be proposed. Law and aesthetics scholarship suggests that certain forms of association and being demand a different legal logic. If this can be understood as making for an ethic
of solidarity, then there is an important conjuncture, even if the
notion of love remains bracketed.

Despite these qualifications, the two bodies of work are similar to the extent that they utilise a style, a way of writing and a
sensibility that rely on aesthetic terms. Unger's relevance for the
project envisaged by this book could best be described as making for a 'politics of the everyday'[11] envisaged in aesthetic
terms. When *Passion* describes the world as 'dense and dark'[12]
it is making use of a literary mode of expression. From the perspective of conventional legal theory such claims would appear
meaningless, general, poetical expressions with no analytical
purchase. However, such a way of writing is meant to suggest
that conventional rigour obscures an essential quality of the
world as lived rather than analysed. The key term in *Politics*, the
notion of negative capability, is an attempt to elaborate this
sense of the lived world. Negative capability does not just
spring from the pages of *Politics* fully formed, but has a pedi-
gree that goes back to Unger's early work, and the idea of
expanded doctrine. Indeed, the importance of negative capability is that it reveals very strongly the aesthetic turn of recent
CLS.

[10] For a consideration of the Greek and Christian traditions of love and their
reinvention see Gearey, A., 'Finnegans Wake and the Law of Love; the Aporia
of Eros and Agape' (1997) 7 *Law and Critique*, 245–67. See also Ch. 6 of the
present work.
[11] Boyle, J., 'Modernist Social Theory: Roberto Unger's *Passion*' (1985) 98
Harvard Law Review 1083.
[12] Unger, n. 2 *supra*, 2.

Expanded doctrine is a critique of a formalism that proposes law as a coherent body of rules that are devoid of politics.[13] *The Critical Legal Studies Movement* argues that doctrine must become enlarged to allow a more thorough linkage between law and politics. Enlarged doctrine is a wilfully contentious category, its boundaries and content difficult to define. At root, though, it provides a challenge to the authority of doctrinal assumptions. Expanded doctrine takes on a specifically aesthetic charge with the idea of negative capability. Negative capability is a delicate notion that needs to be treated with a certain amount of care. The term is first mentioned in a letter by the poet John Keats. Reflecting on his poetry, Keats made a distinction between sensation and thought. This has been interpreted as suggesting a division between the logic and imagination. The most profound truths, 'the holiness of the heart's affections' can be apprehended only through a form of imaginative engagement. What Keats calls 'consequitive reasoning,'[14] the ability to identify, represent and classify, can operate in some important senses, it can measure and describe the world, it can establish mathematical relationships but it lacks the synthetic insight of imagination. Only imagination can see into the heart of things. A further distinction makes reasoning a passive way of ordering, and imagination an active, creative force. What imagination perceives 'must be true—whether or not it existed before'. Whereas reasoning defines, negative capability describes the human capability 'of being in uncertainties, Mysteries, doubts, without any irritable reaching after fact and reason'.[15] In contrast to the man of reason the poet does not need to make up his mind. The poet's mind is 'a thoroughfare for all thoughts'.[16]

There is a risk that serious harm could be done to the notion of negative capability by inserting it into legal or social theory.

[13] Unger, R., *The Critical Legal Studies Movement* (Cambridge, Mass., Harvard University Press, 1986), 565.

[14] Bates, W. J, *Negative Capability* (Cambride, Mass., Harvard University Press, 1939), 25.

[15] *Ibid.*, 43.

[16] *Ibid.*, 26.

It is not to be expected that negative capability is properly articulated and philosophically correct as it represents Keats
attempting to express his own provisional understanding of the
creative processes. The transformation of the idea in *Politics* perhaps says more about Unger's project and the demands of producing a legal aesthetics. The present interpretation of negative
capability will be more concerned with its latter deployment than
in defending the rather stark opposition between thought and
feeling or reason and imagination.

There are two errors that need to be avoided. Negative capability, at least as it appears in *Politics*, is not a thesis about indeterminacy. Although difficult to summarise, this thesis would
hold to the seriously compromised nature of rational justification.
It is easy to appreciate that Keats could be interpreted in this
way, with his privileging of mystery rather than rational discourse. Whether or not this is a sufficient interpretation of Keats'
own understanding of his work is secondary for a legal aesthetics. In *Politics*, there is a clear sense in which negative capability
is linked to a political project. Although this is difficult to define
in conventional terms, it will be shown that negative capability
does present a set of preferred choices for action in the world.
Negative capability is directed at a weakening of the justifications
for the forms of social life that the project opposes.

The second error would be to conceive of negative capability
along the lines proposed by James Boyd White. At first glance,
there is a superficial resemblance between negative capability
and White's idea of literary language, but this comparison is
misconceived. White contrasts legal discourse with literary language, and argues that law can learn a more refined ethical sense
from literature. Negative capability does not have this innate
ethical dimension. This is not to argue, however, that it could
not be co-ordinated with an ethics of political engagement.
Indeed, for Unger negative capability is effectively rethought as
a form of expanded doctrine. It begins to exemplify a way of
thinking and feeling that is not inflexible and restricted but can
be linked to a more vital sense of opposition to the inflexible.
The argument is compressed and needs expanding. In the

105

widest of senses negative capability provides *Politics* with a notion of the imagination as excessive: 'the powers of the mind will never be exhaustively defined' or, to put it a slightly different way, there is a permanent disjuncture between 'insight and available discourse'.[17] Just as insight can exceed forms of expression, no theoretical reflection on human possibility is ever sufficient. There is to be no compromise with the forms and categories of institutional discourse in the way that White's literary ethics appears to propose. There are problems with Unger's work that will be qualified in this chapter, but on the whole it will be preferred to White's approach.

It is also necessary to stress that negative capability is utilised as a notion of production rather than passive reflection. Implicit in this argument is an elaboration of the very idea of poetry. The Greek term *poesis* can be translated as 'the making'. Referring back to Keats' elaboration of negative capability, justifying poetic making is not a realised sense of end product, but the process itself. Keats stresses the extent to which making remains dark, hidden in its own mysteries. It would be wrong to make this process too transparent. Perhaps *Ozymandias*, with its image of the sands of the desert and the association of the act of writing poetry with this endless, shifting placeless place, could provide a metaphor. The aesthete as poet, as maker, evokes a productive energy.

In *Politics*, negative capability as *poesis* is the empowerment that results from the disruption of traditional hierarchies. It relates to an attitude to the self and the projects that one undertakes in the world. Negative capability is a revolution of the everyday, disturbing inflexible patterns of organisation and thought. In another expression that again clearly displays aesthetic leanings, it is an inherently romantic space, where personal encounters allow people to reinvent themselves. Romantic

[17] Unger, R., *False Necessity* (Cambridge, Cambridge University Press, 1987) 20. The other two volumes in the *Politics* trilogy are *Social Theory; Its Situation and Its Task*, considered below, and *Plasticity into Power: Comparative Historical Studies on the Institutional Conditions of Economic and Military Success* (Cambridge, Cambridge University Press, 1987).

is used not so much to indicate a periodisation of art or litera-ture, but to refer to the 'secular romance' and more particularly to a view of the world developed in this form. Romance is an articulation of the 'personal encounter'[18] with the world, its obstacles, triumphs and disappointments. Behind the complex forms of romance, there is the recurrent fascination with the loss and possibility of regaining personal and social arcadias. The romance is, above all, the secular elaboration of the need for a striving towards elusive goals in a difficult world.

Politics imagines the total transformation of the law. This is one of the more problematic aspects of Unger's thought. Total transformation presupposes a coherent and worked-out theory that is adequate to this vision. Does this overestimate the relia-bility of a single programme of reform? More worryingly, the need for coherence and overarching goals may contradict the reliance on negative capability, which suggests a far more cau-tious and tentative approach. To develop this argument, a brief description of Unger's project will be followed by an attempt to re-read and reinvent. Certain aspects must be rejected, but the notion of institutional transformation can be retained and refined.

So as not to overburden this chapter with exegesis and sum-mary, the notion of rights will be seen as both central to a vision of law transformed and the key site for critique. Transformed rights have to be distinguished from the limiting connection with the protection of settled property relations. They can be con-ceptualised as immunity rights, destabilisation rights and soli-darity rights. Although these new rights would not entirely replace property rights, they would contribute to the relocation of power in the community and the disruption of monopolies. Destabilisation rights would accompany immunity rights. The former would protect individuals or groups against applications of governmental power and against any form of exclusion from public decision-making. Immunity rights would also guarantee an adequate amount of welfare protection. Destabilisation rights

[18] n. 2. *supra*, 29.

would be dedicated to the breaking down of hierarchies of power. Alongside destabilisation rights, solidarity rights would 'give legal form to social relations of reliance and trust'.[19] This last group of rights covers a wide field that includes all aspects of 'inter-dependence' and could be built up from principles already existing in the law of fiduciary relations, the contractual doctrines of reliance and the notion of good faith. Popular empowerment would also demand a redistribution of resources. This could take the form of an appropriation of resources by those excluded from the present commercial and financial sources of power. One key proposal is a capital fund on which individuals and groups could make claims.

Must an aesthetics of law fall into the trap of fetishising rights? It is also doubtful whether the political will exists to effect such a massive transformation. However, what underlies this idea of transformed rights does not necessarily become realised in this particular vision.

Unger's work does invite the reader's own reconstruction and re-reading. Indeed, there is an invitation to reinvent the project, to read it differently.[20] The text draws a distinction between two theoretical positions: super theory and ultra theory.[21] The former describes a total social vision that is the ambition of *Politics*. Ultra theory, though, appears closer to the gay science with its stress upon discontinuity. It shares the concern with the overturning of institutions, with deviations from the existing order. Whereas super theory demands a 'big book' to accommodate its

[19] n. 17 *supra*, 535.

[20] This is also encouraged by Unger's recourse to the notion of self revision. See *ibid*. The argument is that, whereas paradigms of thought allow various statements to be made about the world and judged to be true or false, these paradigms simultaneously disallow other interpretations. Nevertheless, a paradigm can never completely determine the combinations of thought and insight that take place within its terms. Indeed, it may be possible to produce insights which 'one may not be able to verify, validate, or even lack sense within established criteria of validity . . .' (at 81) In other words, 'understanding' has the potential to exceed the possibilities offered by discourse.

[21] Unger, R., *Social Theory: its Situation and its Task* (Cambridge, Cambridge University Press, 1987) 165.

studies, ultra theory can take a more open form. Unger states that there is no substantial reason to prefer either style of analysis. Even though he has chosen to practise 'super theory' he 'hope[s] that the ultra theorists are out there working away'.[22] Remaining authentic might mean reading *Politics* as an open text; not a master work demanding adherence, but a provocation that suggests a way forward and invites dissent.

At another point, the text is careful to recommend neither the notion of the total revolution, nor that of quiescence and quietism. The task of thinking is to come to terms with a contemporary location, the failure to 'imagine transformation'. Transformation appears either as a largely inexplicable historical movement or as a catastrophe that overwhelms one set of institutions and produces another virtually indistinguishable structure. People tend to remain quiescent, as a contingent *status quo* appears necessary, or suffer from 'cynical reason'. To move beyond, or even to operate within this impasse is to contend with a number of difficulties.

A starting point would be to recuperate the opposition between life and law, but in a more dynamic form. Looked at more broadly, this is the concern with the relationship between life and the structures that represent and speak for it. How can an ethics or a code ever relate to the complexities of a life lived, whose tensions, loves and deceptions cut across its neat categories? At the same time, it is necessary to bear in mind that life is constantly being judged. The point about ethics, moral codes and life made in Chapter 3 is directly analogous. Life can never simply be lived, it has to be justified, and justification involves standards, rules and laws. Critical thought must not become a naïve anarchism. How, then, should the vision of law transformed be approached?

One has to make use of an idea of endemic conflict or tension that lies beneath any institutional situation.[23] The extent to

[22] n. 21 *supra*, 169.
[23] An interesting reflex to these ideas can be found in the recent work of Joseph Raz. See *Engaging Reason* (Oxford, Oxford University Press, 1999).

which this endemic tension can be manipulated to disturb the assumptions and limits of the context can be investigated. A link can be made between the variability of social entrenchment and the plasticity of the social roles that depend on that context. Entrenched contexts produce social hierarchies that are difficult to change and appear resistant to activities that might disrupt or redefine their *modus operandi*. The relative strengths of any particular interpretative or institutional framework can be gauged by the extent to which they can shape activities and not in turn be shaped. There are prejudices and perspectives inherent to institutions that impose limits on perceptions that would otherwise be open to question. However, even entrenched contexts generate disputes that threaten disruption, an 'endless stream of petty conflicts that may escalate at any moment into more fundamental context-threatening disputes'.[24] Once a context has been disrupted, there is the possibility that another context could generate itself.[25] Contexts are thus conditional. Although a particular context could be powerful enough to mandate a normative vision of the social world it could never be said that it was impervious to challenge.

Disentrenchment is not simply an activity for its own sake. To be empowered, individuals have to live in circumstances of mutual trust.[26] The issue is the extent to which conflicts can produce changes in the law; the extent to which the institution of the law is open to interruption or doomed to repeat entrenched social and legal relationships. *Politics'* essential contribution is thus the notion of the precariousness of context. Context is always open to change. It can never preserve itself absolutely. Opposition, in this sense, is inescapable. It is a product of the inherent instability of any system. Rather than a manifesto for total change, this is a possible thinking of local interventions, of making use of a context inherently unstable.

[24] Unger, n. 17 *supra*, 5.

[25] *Ibid.*, 9. There is also the possibility that the old context could reassert itself. As the gay science might suggest, the outcome depends on the relative strength of the opposing forces.

[26] n. 2 *supra*, 74.

This interpretation of Unger's project reveals the influence of the gay science. The gay science makes for a similar study of passionate attachments and commitments and their interaction with the legal forms that are meant to represent them and speak for them.[27] It recommends a particular engagement with alchemic[28] properties of the ideas developed so far.

Comunismo libertario: communism and the common law

It is now necessary to work this through with reference to legal doctrine. A string of appellate authorities will be examined that concern the so-called family assets doctrine.[29] The conflicts in these cases can be understood in terms of the tensions produced by changing notions of work, the matrimonial relationship and ownership of property. In the language of disentrenchment, the cases raise the question of how law can both sustain and change contexts. Previously gender roles had seemed 'stabilised', effectively shaping the social world and producing defining structures of hierarchy and authority. A regime of property law interfaced with a social situation where husbands worked and wives remained at home. Title to property was registered in the husband's name. A stabilised social context could be said to 'disappear' to the extent that it becomes accepted and society identifies with it completely. Thus, a regime of property law becomes one of the context of daily routines. Behind these forms lurk a further set of considerations. From a sociological perspective the household is a major focus of economic activity. As has been pointed out, in the modern era the household is not a

[27] The Nietzschean enemy without which the self would not appear recurs in the location of the self as the social self: see *ibid.*, p. vii.

[28] On the alchemic properties of words and other chemicals see Virr, P., 'Three Poems' (2000) 5 *Law Text Culture* 1. See also Virr, P., *The Dead Title*, forthcoming.

[29] Although the following discussion makes use of the term family assets, it should not be seen as a privileging of heterosexuality as the definition of the family unit. The conclusions to be drawn should apply equally to a relationship characterised by mutual trust and cooperation.

unit of production as it was for home workers before the industrial revolution; it is a place of consumption. The household is the place where both goods and services are effectively distributed. In a society where marriage is still to some extent the foundation of the household and the family, the regime of property ownership between spouses is of fundamental importance for the distribution of financial and social capital.[30] To what extent can the law assist in the production of equitable arrangements?

Rimmer v. *Rimmer*, *Fribance* v. *Fribance* and *Ulrich* v. *Ulrich* are cases similar on their facts and concern difficult questions of property distribution on divorce. Taken as a group they suggest that the law does not just restrict and confirm entrenched assumptions. In doctrinal terms *Rimmer*, *Fribance* and *Ulrich* represent an interruption of the categories of property law. In Otto Kahn-Freund's phrase a 'communistic' interpretation of property suddenly appears within the common law.[31]

The law in these cases is somewhat complicated. In summary, as the matrimonial home was in the husband's name it was difficult for the wife to establish title or an interest in the property. Prior to the Matrimonial Proceedings and Property Act 1970[32] property distribution was controlled by normal principles of law. The law obscured the extent to which the wife's domestic duties enabled the husband to work and pay off the mortgage. Although the law had sustained this context, *Rimmer*, *Fribance* and *Ulrich* suggest that law is not impermeable to experiment. After a brief summary of the salient facts, the reasoning and outcomes of these cases will be examined.

In *Rimmer* v. *Rimmer*,[33] Mrs Rimmer provided the deposit and the remainder of the purchase money was raised by a mortgage in the husband's name. The house was conveyed into the husband's name. Whilst Mr Rimmer was away on active war service, Mrs. Rimmer paid off a proportion of the mortgage

---

[30] Kahn-Freund, O., in Freidman, W.G. (ed.), *Matrimonial Property Law* (London, Stevnes, 1955), 267–314.

[31] *Ibid.*, 267.

[32] Now the Matrimonial Causes Act 1973.

[33] *Rimmer* v. *Rimmer* [1952] 2 All E.R. 863.

from the housekeeping money which he had provided. She also contributed from her own resources. An application to the court was made on the breakdown of the relationship to determine the distribution of respective entitlements to the matrimonial home. The registrar thought that shares should be divided in arithmetical proportion to contributions. On appeal the county court judge decided that the interests in the house were determined at the moment of purchase. Although the wife had provided the deposit, the husband had become liable for the entire mortgage, and the shares should reflect this initial distribution. The Court of Appeal held that the proceeds of the sale should be divided in equal shares.

Fribance v. *Fribance*[34] is another case concerned with title to matrimonial property that took place against the background of the war. Whilst Mr Fribance was in the air force and making an allocation of his earnings, Mrs Fribance went out to work. Her earnings were used to pay the household expenses. Mr Fribance's earnings were largely saved. When they bought the freehold of the property in which they had been living, Mrs Fribance contributed £20, a sum was raised by a mortgage and the remainder of the amount was provided from Mr Fribance's savings. The property was placed in the husband's name. When the relationship broke down, a summons was issued to determine the ownership of the property. The registrar decided that it belonged in the main to the husband and the wife was entitled to a share that represented her initial £20 contribution. The county court decided that it belonged to them in equal shares and the Court of Appeal upheld this decision.

Ulrich v. *Ulrich*[35] is somewhat different. Before the couple were married, but whilst they were engaged, a property was purchased. Mrs Ulrich provided the deposit from her savings and also covered certain disbursements. The remainder of the purchase price was raised by a mortgage. Although the husband did not provide any cash, the mortgage was in his name, and the

[34] *Fribance* v. *Fribance* [1957] 1 All E.R. 357.
[35] *Ulrich* v. *Ulrich and Fenton* [1968] 1 All E.R. 67.

conveyance was also taken in his name. Both husband and wife worked, although the wife took some time off to care for their child and then resumed working. The relationship broke down on account of the wife's adultery and the husband left the matrimonial home. The Court of Appeal held that neither party should be punished, and that the court would determine the distribution of the proceeds from the sale of the property on the basis of fairness. It was eventually divided into half shares.

What characterises these judgments is a search for a response that does justice to the situation rather than resting on the repetition of conventional legal principles. Although Parliament has legislated, no 'principles had been laid down for the guidance of the courts'.[36] Responding means law's intervention in the kind of relationship that had traditionally been left unregulated in the private sphere. From where can the principle of judgement be derived?

Rimmer v. *Rimmer* and *Fribance* v. *Fribance* can be analysed together. Sir Raymond Evershed MR's reasoning in *Rimmer* v. *Rimmer* begins with the difficulties that arise when the court has to do justice between two people whose marriage has come to an end. The duty of the court is to remain sensitive to the details of each case. Referring to *Re Roger's Question*,[37] Evershed MR approaches a sensitive task. The job of the judge is to divine what was in the minds of the parties, and then to make an order that reflects what the parties would have intended at the time of the transaction; the court has to decide an issue on a 'hypothesis which does not exist'.[38] This is the judge as the hero of the gay science, the one who has to invent a morality only partially guided

[36] *Supra*, n. 33, 868.

[37] *Re Roger's Question* [1948] 1 All ER 328 was an important case. Both husband and wife were claiming that it was originally intended that beneficial ownership should be completely vested in the latter. The husband subsequently alleged that the property was his, subject only to an obligation to repay the wife for a small amount of money borrowed to pay a tenth of the purchase price. Both the husband's and the wife's claims were rejected by the county court judge, who interpreted the 'tiff' as suggesting that each was to have contributed to the original price of the house in the shares that they did indeed contribute.

[38] n. 33 *supra*, 864.

by what the tradition can offer. There is, first of all, a failure of the idea of contract. There can be no contract between husband and wife as domestic arrangements fall outside the jurisdiction of property law. If this kind of contract were justiciable, the pure domestic world would be invaded by the harshness of the law. In *Balfour* v. *Balfour*[39] it was said that the relationship between husband and wife could only ever be one of honour: 'natural love and affection . . . counts for so little in these cold courts'.[40] Before we look at the resolution of this problem, the similarities with *Fribance* need to be noted.

In *Fribance* v. *Fribance*, the husband's argument had relied on a line of cases that included *Hoddinott* v. *Hoddinott*[41] and *Balfour* v. *Balfour*. His counsel argued that the wife's claim must fail as the house was in the husband's name, and she could not show that there was a gift, a contract or a trust. *Balfour* was then relied upon to show that, even if there was an agreement rather than a formal contract, it was a domestic agreement that could not give rise to a legal action for breach. In *Fribance*, Denning LJ boldly doubted whether such a line of argument was 'valid today'.[42] A wife does not have to prove that there is a contract. So much would follow from Romer LJ in *Rimmer* when he asserted that 'legal principles' required modification in the event of their application to disputes between husbands and wives. But matters did not rest there.

To return to the reasoning of *Balfour*, the court said that even though domestic agreements could not be sued upon, what one does find in the home is a form of 'quasi law'. This is described as a 'domestic code' where husband and wife are 'advocates, judges, courts, sheriff's officer and reporter'. Indeed, it is a jurisdiction that defines the home as a place apart, a 'domain' where the 'king's writ does not seek to run'.[43] In *Balfour* this is used to support the argument that there can be no cause of action in contract for an agreement made between a husband and a wife.

---

[39] *Balfour* v. *Balfour* [1918–19] All E.R. 860.
[40] *Ibid.*, 579.
[41] *Hoddinott* v. *Hoddinott* [1949] 2 K.B. 406.
[42] *Fribance*, n. 34 *supra*, 359.
[43] *Balfour*, n. 39 *supra*, 579.

However, in *Fribance*, this argument is turned around. Why is this? The court appreciates that merely stressing the inviolability of the social space would make for injustice. What can be done? In the failure of contract, the court appears to defer to the jurisdiction of the relationship, the place of the 'domestic code'. This code affirms that an obligation arises between people when they commit themselves to each other. It is a 'quasi law' whose source is the intimate relationship itself. This jurisdiction matches that of the courts in a shadowy form. Although it does not publish reports of its decisions, there is still a kind of spectral jurisdiction and there are principles on which the court can draw. The task of the court is to give form to the principles of this quasi law. *Fribance* could be read *contra Balfour* as an attempt to make love and affection figure in the cold common law courts.

On what legal resource can the court draw to give legal form to the law of the heart? The case law prior to *Rimmer* v. *Rimmer* established that section 17 of the Married Women's Property Act of 1882 contained a wide power to achieve what was just and fair between the parties. Although this could not, of course, enable a judge to make an order that contradicted established rules of law, property disputes between husbands and wives could be dealt with in a fairly robust way. The starting point was that property in a married relationship should be used in common, irrespective of the question of who owned the property. This user-ship in common could influence the disposition of the property on the break-up of the marriage. As far as Denning LJ is concerned in *Rimmer*, the case is an opportunity to restate a doctrine that was rejected in *Hoddinott* v. *Hoddinott*:

> if the husband and wife together embark on a joint venture in which they equally contribute their skill, then if nothing is said between them, the proper inference is that the proceeds go to them jointly.[44]

Denning LJ's defence of his principle refers to the discretion under the Act as structured by the law. He also makes reference to a principle that falls into the 'domestic code'. Questions between husband and wife should be resolved not by 'dictation

[44] *Hoddinott*, n. 41 *supra*, 415, rephrased in *Rimmer*, n. 33, 869 *supra*.

116

of one to the other', but 'by agreement, by give and take'.[45] This does not detract from the usual principles that would mean that title depends on the property bought and who bought it, but it raises the presumption that if money is invested or property bought in joint names, it should belong to the parties jointly. 'Family assets' could thus be defined as 'the things intended to be a continuing provision for them during their joint lives'. The potential reach of the doctrine is radical as it does not depend on their allocation of spending and resources, but extends over assets held for joint benefit.

The doctrine appears to offer a robust way of resolving this kind of dispute. Moreover, it does not seem to operate in a way that would license a kind of moral economy that replaces a more formal legal regime. Consider the problem of the wife's adultery in *Ulrich* v. *Ulrich*. The wife appears demonised: '[t]he husband forgave the wife's adultery on one occasion and tried to make the marriage work for the sake of the child. Really if ever there was a case where the wife brought the marriage to an end, this was it'.[46] After the relationship had broken down, the wife terminated her affair with the co-respondent. 'She goes out to work earning money herself. So she is a woman on her own, going out to work, having the child at home'.[47] As has been pointed out, there are assumptions about gender that condition these judgments.[48] But this case develops in an interesting way.[49] One

[45] *Ibid.*, 416.

[46] Ulrich, n. 35 *supra*, 69.

[47] *Ibid.*, 69.

[48] See Bottomley, A., 'Self and Subjectivities: Languages of Claim in Property Law' (1986) 20 *Journal of Law and Society* 56.

[49] At the same time, it is not to deny that there are gender assumptions operating in these cases: for instance, the whole discourse of the 'good wife' in *Balfour* and *Hoddinott*, whose economy of thrift and saving supports the 'husband's earnings' (n. 41, *supra*, at 416). *Re Roger's Question* is also relevant here. In this case the wife had a capital of £500, and had refused to provide any indemnity to the husband . In the words of the court she 'could not have her cake and eat it too' (at 330). On the facts as perceived by the court, the wife never assumed liability for nine tenths of the mortgage and thus could not be assumed to have a larger interest in the house. One has to bear in mind that it would be a mistake to see the associative space as one undistorted by conflict.

might have thought that this would mean that the judge was not sympathetic to the woman, after all she is responsible for the collapse of the marriage, and she is the one who now works and leaves the child in another's care. At a narrative level, the stage might now be set for the punishment of a woman who not only breaks up her marriage but also wants more than her fair share. However, the court held that the proceeds of the sale of the matrimonial home should be divided in such a non-punitive way. It was thought that the wife should get back 'approximately' the money that she had invested as the case stands 'on a par with all the marriage cases'.[50] Section 17 cannot be used in a penal way, it cannot punish 'a guilty wife'.[51] The court has an obligation to be fair in all the circumstances that pertain to the case.

If one accepts that the law is not operating in these cases merely as a way of furthering a patriarchal ideology, it is still necessary to show how this reading is unusual. How does this analysis differ from a more conventional argument that law can change with the times? For a start, what is being examined here is a heretical line of cases, a disturbance in doctrine before the more conventional principles of property law reasserted themselves in the cases of *Pettitt* v. *Pettitt* and *Gissing* v. *Gissing*.[52] *Gissing* and *Pettitt* present the law returned to correctness after deviation and error. It was held that section 17 of the Married Women's Property Act did not contain a power to alter title to property, merely a narrow procedural device that could not be interpreted so broadly.

The very cases that killed the family assets doctrine do not entirely resolve the issues that emerge in its wake. It is as if, once law turns away from this radical intervention, it cannot quite recover its equipoise. As this is not a discourse on the law of trusts or matrimonial property, it is necessary only to trace the contours of a couple of a representative doctrinal problem. After the death of the family assets doctrine, one way in which an

[50] Ulrich, n. 35 *supra*, 70.

[51] *Ibid.*, 71.

[52] *Pettitt* v. *Pettitt* [1969] 2 All ER 385, *Gissing* v. *Gissing* [1970] 2 All ER 780.

interest in property might be claimed for the non-property-holding spouse was through finding that the property was held under a trust. The problem rests on ascertaining the circumstances when a husband is to become a trustee for his wife. There could, of course, be a formal agreement, though this would be rare in the kind of case with which we are concerned. If there was no formal trust, an imputed trust can arise. This could be inferred from conduct, but a judge could not 'invent' an imputed trust. The only certain way to find a trust would be to find that a party had made contributions that were referable to the purchase of the property. Although it is unclear how referable these contributions need to be, if the contributions are indirect, it would be unlikely to give rise to an interest in the property. A great deal rests, then, on this distinction between direct and indirect contributions.

The problem remaining is how this distinction is sustained. If one objects to the elements of discretion that the family assets doctrine gave the courts, this problem is hardly resolved here. The court still has discretion whether or not to discover the existence of a trust on the evidence given. Moreover, whereas the family assets doctrine apparently resisted a moralistic interpretation, after its demise the law effectively encourages dishonesty and subterfuge. Under the family assets doctrine, the facts of the break-up of the relationship did not effect the distribution of property. Now, however, the 'candid and honest wife' might 'agree that the matter was never discussed', whereas a 'more sophisticated' wife, with knowledge of the law and before a 'sympathetic judge' might be able to turn 'vague evidence' into evidence of an agreement. [53]

What conclusions can be drawn from this? Rather than the coherent development of rules and principles, law may appear as a conflicting set of materials. At any given point, argument can cut into the law and offer to reassemble it in such a way as to produce a disentrenchment of solidified rules. Forms of social relationship that develop in the world outside the law provoke

[53] *Gissing* v. *Gissing*, n. 52 *supra*, 783.

these occasions for intervention. No doubt, law is not of a piece. Different fields of law will have concepts that are more or less malleable. What this particular study shows is that, at least in this important interface between property and passion, there is a possibility that the law itself can be interrupted and developed in a way that offers protection for those who commit themselves to a relationship of intimate trust. What hampers any definitive discussion of this issue is the necessarily open nature of the processes of disentrenchment discussed. A provisional conclusion would be that law is always in a more or less problematic situation. Future disputes will continue to offer further opportunities for the law to disentrench itself.[54]

Recent scholarship provides further support for the disentrenchment thesis. The disturbance caused by the family assets doctrine has led to a search for an alternative way of thinking the community of property at common law. That resources can be found to further this communitarian thesis suggests that law has the potential to develop differently. If family assets simply appeared as a doctrinal category, only to be erased and leave no trace in case law or more broadly in legal scholarship, then law might only ever be thought of as context-preserving. Research on family property is intriguing because it returns to the notion of the emotional reality of the intimate relationship. The approach of the judges in both the cases that gave birth to the doctrine and those that laid it to rest is criticised. In the former, the judges commit a serious mistake in looking to the thinking of the parties in seeking to establish a way of showing that property should be held in common. In the latter cases, the judges commit the same mistake when they argue that the presence of a trust should depend on the parties' conceptions of how property was to be held.

These approaches fundamentally misunderstand the reality of a relationship that is built on mutual trust and not clear thinking about respective property rights. But how might the law take

---

[54] For continuing difficulties caused by the family assets doctrine, see *Midland Bank* v. *Cooke* [1995] 2 FLR 915.

into account an emotional rather than a business relationship? One might draw on the law of unjust enrichment. Although the law in this area is markedly individualistic, there is a potential that it could become more focused on values of trust and mutual aid. If the law of unjust enrichment proves resistant to this development, then there may be a different approach that defends communality of property. This approach, then, is based on the concept of a fiduciary relationship. A concept primarily applied to commercial relationships could with certain modifications, be adapted for service within a family context as the core value of trust and collaboration is clearly transferable. A fiduciary holds property for another, utilising any benefit drawn from the property for the benefit of the other rather than himself. In dealings with the property, the fiduciary would have to take into account the wishes of the beneficiary. The flexibility of this concept is such that it need not just apply to the matrimonial relationship; its extension to any relationship where property benefits people communally is conceivable. A further modification of the doctrine would allow any form of contribution to be seen as significant in giving rise to a fiduciary relationship. If the conclusion is that 'much is already in place'[55] then this transformation of legal doctrine has the further benefit of not demanding the total transformation of the law recommended by *Politics*.

There are some necessary further reflections on the nature of this legal analysis. A gay science of law would draw our attention to an understanding of the disputes themselves, which can too easily be seen as simply a backdrop for a legal decision. These conflicts are to be viewed more properly as provocations to the law. Feminist legal analysis has made this point in the past, but perhaps the necessary focus should not be on the man or the woman, but on the space they create between them, the space of their relationship: the separator that unites, the space of passion. In the terms of the gay science it is the essential enigma, the 'puzzle' that constitutes the intimate relationship. Nietzsche's text,

---

[55] Gardner, S., 'Rethinking Family Property', (1993) 109 *Law Quarterly Review* 229–371.

when it adopts the position of the 'moralist', who seeks to analyse, categorise and discuss this enigma is similar to the law when it invents the doctrine of family assets. The law is forced to talk about what cannot be understood, only created.[56] Thus law takes part in the invention of a form that can protect the arrangements that are made between people. The family assets doctrine produces a legal concept that disrupts the canonical, and in this sense oppressive, concept that ownership depends on title. In the moment of decision, the law takes a risk.[57]

Looking back on the ends of the law

The injunction placed upon the critical legal interpreter is to find the spaces where doctrine stumbles, where legal principles can become shaped to fit social realities, rather than simply repeating a legal logic. This call to arms stresses the inseparability of legal theory, legal practice and political vision. It heralds the coming of the lawyer as existential hero whose activity transforms both her and her world. As *Politics* makes clear, to think of law in these terms means to move away from the nineteenth-century ideas of the lawyer as public servant, or even the more contemporary ideas of the lawyer in private practice providing a service to her clients. The ideology of professionalism can too easily provide a smokescreen that obscures both difficult individual choices and wider concerns about the role of law itself. The lawyer as technician, as supporter of and apologist for the *status quo* applying objective and determinate rules to the facts of social disputes can no longer be sustained. For a start, most people simply do not accept this as an adequate representation of the law. At a more sophisticated level, the 'formalism and objectivity' which underpin this vision of law's neutrality have been devastated by critique.

[56] See Drakopoulou, M., 'Women's Resolutions of Lawes Reconsidered: Epistemic Shifts and the Emergence of Feminist Legal Discourse, (2000) 11 *Law and Critique* 47–71.

[57] The Law Commission is presently researching the issue of property rights for home sharers, the research to be published in 2001.

The lawyer needs to be imagined as a kind of culture hero who is involved in struggle as a means of changing both the intimate and public conditions of social existence. To accept the vocation of the lawyer is not merely to enter a job. The lawyer 'accepts the spiritual authority of that characteristically modern and even modernist ideal: you affirm your worth, in part, by attempting to change some aspect of society and culture'.[58] Identity is created in just such an ability to stand apart from determining conditions. For this position to make sense the discourse of law has to be understood in a certain way. The legal text does not appear as a repository of immemorial truths, but as a site in which ideological disputes can be fought out; the text itself carries 'radically inconsistent'[59] ideas that can be creatively worked at to elaborate accounts of human association. Formalism's closed categories legitimised the law and provided support for the idea of coherence but failed to insulate law from political dispute.

Just as the aesthete must create themselves with the available materials, radical legal argument must make use of existing resources. If expanded doctrine is a way of writing and arguing that crosses genres, that brings the insights of other disciples to bear on law, its condition of possibility is the imagination of the lawyer herself. Here is passion writ large; it returns to the pervasive theme of the excessiveness or context-breaking aspect of personality that provides something like an ontology of the human subject. For Sartre the most complete human being was Che Guevara; Unger's evocation hopefully avoids this kind of idolisation, whilst stressing human potential. To be most alive is merely to realise the potential of the everyday, as it is here that one becomes 'an active and conscious participant in the conflict over the terms of collective life'.[60] Underlying this conception is the belief that society is an artifact, that social order is the product of struggles.

[58] Unger, n. 17 *supra*, 668.
[59] *Ibid.*, 572.
[60] *Ibid.*, 670.

To make use of an expression discussed in Chapter 2, it is a practice of hope and faith. Projects informed by negative capability are thus not informed by a strong sense of teleology, of the ultimate achievement of something like a socialist utopia. They are interventions that are directed by a sense that law needs to serve the desires of people to exist in conditions of mutual trust and solidarity. These interventions may be inspired by imaginative engagements with utopian thinking, but they are also local, small-scale and not justified by one single overarching programme. Legal aesthetics would accept that life in law is defined by principles and rules that determine and restrain interpretative activity and political possibility, but it would see this as the challenge to the joyous interpreter: make it new.

6
The Recording Angel

We are in pursuit of a style of thinking. Circling back to the beginning of the book, this section offers a closing interpretation of Shelley's assertion that poets are the unacknowledged legislators of the world. It has already been argued that a poet should not impose a morality through his poetry. Moral standards are always specific and limited to a time and place. What, then, is the poet's legislation? There are some suggestions in Shelley's translation of Plato's *Ion*, a text contemporary with *A Defence of Poetry*.[1] *Ion* describes the poet's 'plumes of rapid imaginings', inventions that go beyond constraining context. It is perhaps another attempt to capture the phantom nature of poetry. Although this use of poetic imagination could be co-ordinated with the idea of disentrenchment developed in the last chapter, there is a further issue that needs to be faced. Context-breaking needs to be informed by an idea of a broader purpose. How could this purpose be defined? Argument will focus on Shelley's *Ode to Liberty* as a poem that remains in dialogue with *Ozymandias* and the other concerns of this book.

Discussion of the authority of law rests largely on questions of its legitimacy, which in turn reflect concerns with the liberty of individuals to realise their lives. Of course, this is part of a much wider debate that can only be touched upon here. One could speak as an anarchist: liberty has nothing to do with the law of the state, but describes freely chosen mutual obligation. Alternatively, liberty could describe the foundation of the law: fundamental liberties restraining arbitrary power and enabling the flourishing of civil society. The word also carries associations

[1] See Notopoulos, J., *The Platonism of Shelley* (Durham, N.C., Duke University Press, 1949), 473.

of free-will. To be liberated is not to be determined; it is to act on grounds that one freely and rationally chooses. None of these senses of the word will be adequate to assist us with the reading of the poem. The reader will come to see that liberty could be what constrains us. Liberty is a law that cannot be avoided. In this sense, there are certain correspondences with the Greek notion of *moirai* elaborated in Chapter 4. We are all subject to fate, but fate is radically open. There is no guarantee that liberty will manifest itself in any time or context, but in some times, in some places, liberty will make her demands known.[2] The concern with the irresistible force of eros is also helpful as liberty compels us to act for reasons we cannot entirely determine.

Ode to Liberty will be presented as a piece that attempts to combine reason and revelation in an original myth of the compulsion to give voice to the law, or the *logos* of liberty. Just as Christian culture had appropriated classical ideas, Shelley saw himself as amalgamating Christian ideas with a theory and practice of art that had both classical and personal dimensions. Shelley's Christianity, however, is profoundly heretical. His logos of liberty does not follow a Christian teleology, and is perhaps not even a thinking of spirit. It is a celebration of surprise.

A little more exposition is necessary if the poem is to be correctly understood as an imaginative engagement with the foundations of the western legal tradition. Shelley's *Ode* indicates the diverse influences of Roman, Greek and Christian thought on western law. The Greek and Roman traditions tended to locate the source of law in reason or nature. Later on, the Christian tradition found the law in the revelation of a God who was removed from creation. Monotheism thus marked a profound break with the pagan world. It placed God at the centre of a universe from which the created order emanated. This articulation of law as *logos* presented a significant break with classical culture, whilst, in other ways, redeploying its tools. The Christians

---

[2] In another text, Shelley explicitly co-ordinates liberty with the idea of chance. See notes on Queen Mab, in *The Poetical Works of Shelley* (Oxford, Oxford University Press, 1952), 810.

codified revelation in the Bible, in the same way that classical culture had its own canonical myths. At the same time, there is a step beyond in the Christian articulation of the law. Law is no longer defined as the good, but as an orientation to what was beyond the civic and transcended the natural. In the Gospels, this is described as the new law, or the law of love. It expressed both God's love for Man, Man's love for God and a love for others. The law of love maintains this sense in which it comes through revelation; it happens as an inbreaking, an overturning of the secular order and good sense. It would be impossible to say that the law of love had been achieved in a positive form, and also presumptuous to give up the search for the form that recognised this ultimate provocation. Shelley's appropriation of Christian thought combines the excessiveness of revelation with a refusal to subscribe to a monotheistic deity. The human imagination, expressing itself in art, is the power that produces gods.

How are these ideas realised in the poem? The *Ode to Liberty* might appear to be based on the literary device of apostrophe, the direct address that summons into presence. However, it soon becomes clear in the first stanza that the poet cannot call Liberty. Liberty determines its own coming. The poet must wait for the great voice of Liberty to begin. He will faithfully record its words, but the poem is not in the poet's control, he is merely the recording angel, the conduit through whic Liberty's message will pass. Liberty, then, cannot be identified with the autonomy of the writer. It might appear that this great celebration of Liberty is the praise of a more profound compulsion. Liberty may come and go; the poet is truly subject to this sovereign power. Engaging with the poem, the reader comes to appreciate that Liberty manifests itself only to disappear. The poem is a record of a trace, an echo ever receding. Under the name of Liberty Shelley is writing in praise of what he cannot adequately describe. For all its importance to literary canon, the *Ode to Liberty* is a poem that fails its own title.

This has to be borne in mind as one engages with specific stanzas and images. At the beginning Liberty appears to be identified with the poem itself:

> . . . From its station in the Heaven of fame
> The Spirit's whirlwind rapt it, and the ray
> Of the remotest sphere of living flame
> Which paves the void was from behind it flung,
> As foam from a ship's swiftness, when there came
> A voice out of the deep: I will record the same.[3]

These lines might appear as mere bombast, a poetry of huge gestures and over-wrought images. But this bombast is a valid poetic strategy. It is best approached through a reading that can make use of the psychoanalytic register, yet resists the idea that psychoanalysis can reduce the mystery of the poem to any essential residue. Recall the images in the lines above. It is difficult to relate them to any concrete ideas. What, for instance, is the 'Spirit's whirlwind' other than the evocation of some mighty and nameless force. Why is the flame 'living'? No doubt one could discover Platonic allusions in these lines that might help elucidate Shelley's thinking, but perhaps it is most interesting to approach this as an attempt to name what cannot be named, to forefront this as a purely creative, fictioning act.

The *Ode* begins with revolution. Liberty is the name of the Spanish revolt, the sudden lightning that breaks apart the old order. To follow the Lacanian formula introduced in Chapter 2 would be to suggest that this insurrection is the interruption of the real. The real always returns to disturb the symbolic order, challenging the fantasm that it had mandated as the foundation of the social. In its place, the real provokes another fantastic representation of social order. The new order will create its own symbols of legitimacy. However, the strange quality of the real is that it both resists and demands its articulation. What is the poem's relation to this event? Shelley desires to give the real a form, to name it Liberty. Note that this is but a repetition of the question one always asks: *Che voui?* What does the other want of me? How can I find my place in the symbolic order? The other, of course, always remains silent. It can never answer the question that one asks of it. This is because the other is 'barred',

---

[3] T. Webb (ed.), *Selected Poems of Shelley* (London, Everyman, 1977), 91.

created through the very desire that must defer it and make it unobtainable. The only solution is for the subject to take responsibility for their desire, to act like Antigone. *Ode to Liberty* also communicates strangely with the image of the whirlwind in Sappho, the wild force of the 'must'. In this stanza, then, Shelley's language is attempting to grant to itself the fantastic force that lies behind any symbolic order. Liberty is the name of this activity. Shelley's language has no ultimate referent to a world out there, but must figure its own power to create a world. Its tragedy, and it is a tragedy anticipated in the watery metaphor that will be expanded presently, is that this repeats the impossibility of signifying the real. Poetry must engage with what escapes; the real will always return to shatter the best laid plans. The waves will close over Shelley's head.

If the real is always surprising; it is part of a materiality that can never be adequately represented, that will always exceed form. In Shelleyan terms this is linked with a doctrine of art and the act of writing itself. These themes are best exemplified in the poem's representation of the primal birth from chaos:

> The sun and serenest Moon sprang forth;
> The burning stars of the abyss were hurled
> Into the depths of Heaven. The deadal earth,
> That island in the ocean of the world
> Hung in the cloud of all sustaining air.[4]

Echoes of Blake's Tyger, that other great evocation of a creator who may be hiding behind his creation, can be heard in these lines. If Blake's poem sets his own creative act, his own bringing into being of a tiger as an act of human creativity against that of God, the Liberty that Shelley is trying to summon makes a similar claim. Note how the image in the *Ode* inverts the expected sense of a Biblical creation scene. Rather than the process beginning with the creation of heaven by a God outside creation who then goes on to create earth and the abyss, the abyss is hurled into heaven. This would appear to give priority to hell rather than heaven. The strange description 'the depths

4 *Ibid.*, 91.

of heaven' also departs from the usual phrase. The reader would expect 'the depths of hell', a spatial metaphor that is rooted in the sense of a creator removed and above fallen and debased matter. What is also interesting about this creation scene is that there is no mention of a transcendent principle. Creation creates itself. It appears to be purely material.

Why is the earth daedal? The word is derived from the name of the mythical character Deadalus, builder of the labyrinth and a personification of the notion of craft and artifice.[5] It is fitting that his spirit should preside over this world. The daedal world is imagined by Shelley as a provocation to create. He has usurped God, he has represented a world created from nothing; he has figured the ultimate creative act. This feeds into the later verse:

> . . . Art, which cannot die,
> With divine wand traced on our earthly home
> Fit imagery to pave Heaven's everlasting dome.[6]

Art both creates and justifies the world. It takes on the immortality traditionally reserved for divinity. The sense of 'everlasting' is not that of an eternal heaven, heaven is 'paved', brought down to earth, by a creative process that has created it. Art is located in the human soul's 'deepest deep', a metaphor which picks up and continues the sense of the materiality of this power.

The poem moves from the creation of the world to the invention of human community. When man appears he is described ironically as 'imperial'. Imperial man is immediately subject to judgement 'under the pavilion/Of the Sun's throne'. Less than sovereign, man is first of all undifferentiated from nature. After leaving behind the state of nature, man becomes subject to tyrants, but this is a stage in a process that appears to lead to a measure of autonomy. Man becomes able to impose a rule of order to which both the natural world and the world of men

---

[5] For a further consideration of Daedalus and conjunctions with law and psychoanalysis see Gearey, A., 'Stephen Dedalus' Magic Words' in Manderson, D. (ed.), *Courting Death* (London, Pluto Press, 1999), 194–216.

[6] Shelley, n. 3 *supra*, 94.

become subject. The seventh stanza puts this in a particularly striking way. Order 'rends' the 'veil of time and space'; order allows differentiation and measurement. It draws the line between nature and culture. Liberty's progress is then traced through classical and Christian culture to the present day. Each form that Liberty takes suffers a fall, only to come again in a different time and place. Consider, for example, the following evocation of Athens:

Within the surface of Time's fleeting river
Its wrinkled image lies, as then it lay,
Immovably unquiet, and for ever
It trembles, but it cannot pass away.[7]

Athens may be an image of the good city, but this is only one expression. It is swept away by the river of time. However, it is the very reflection of Liberty in the surface of the river that perpetuates the image. Liberty is preserved in a medium that both perpetuates it and destroys it. To follow this argument to its end one would lead to a consideration of the tension between the representation of history as a ceaseless ongoing movement, and the evocation of Liberty as a recurrent demand. Time's fleeting river embodies one sense of time: swift, fleeting, historical time. The evocation of Liberty, however, takes place in and against this linear time as a form of repetition. It would be very difficult to read this poem as the progress of an essential rationality that organises and gives form to reason. A kind of repetition is affirmed.

As explained in the *Book of Sand*, eternal recurrence repeats the form of the decision: do you fall into despair, or 'have you experienced a tremendous moment'? One would have to answer the following question in the affirmative: '[d]o you desire this once more and innumerable times more?'[8] Liberty is a repetition of the urge to affirmation. Shelley accepts the risk that any content of Liberty will fail, will collapse with an interruption of the real; yet attempts to articulate Liberty must continue:

[7] *Ibid.*, 93.
[8] *Ibid.*, 274.

What if the earth can clothe and feed
Amplest millions at their need,
And power in thought be that as the tree within the seed?
Or what if Art, an ardent intercessor,
Driving on fiery wings to Nature's throne,
Checks the great mother stooping to caress her,
And cries' Give me, thy child, dominion
Over all heights and depth?' Life can breed
New wants, and wealth from those who toil and groan,
Rend, of thy gifts and hers, a thousandfold for one![9]

Two questions structure this passage: 'what if . . . Or what if'. 'If' holds open the possibility of difference, it suggests that events could always arrange themselves differently.[10] The repetition of these questions suggests that the failures of the past must not destroy a sense of possibility, a sense of the openness and contingency of history. One must therefore think oneself equal to the greatest events of the past, an act of faith that privileges the human imagination. It returns in a strong sense to the notion of poet as legislator. If this is a manifesto, its only demand is to make the original demand. It is as if this act of thought founds and justifies itself. This is the active need to over-reach, to 'conquer', and to deny the past in the name of the future.

As the stanza above suggests, Liberty is not an escape from judgement; it is the realisation of a form of judgement. Interestingly, this can only emerge when a certain kind of thinking comes to an end. Shelley figures it as the fall of the last priest. This metaphor should not distract from the more engaging thoughts that follow:

---

[9] *Ibid.*, 97.

[10] This stanza presents the image of a female lawgiver. Liberty compels Art to address Nature, who is his mother. Her prior dominion is presupposed by his request. There is a request for a kind of equilibrium, a fair return. There is a complex set of concerns that have to be worked out. Why should this question of Liberty's articulation be connected to a female figure? Can Liberty be articulated through some notion of economy, some kind of distributive justice?

Till human thoughts might kneel alone,
Each before the judgement throne
Of its own aweless soul, or that Power unknown![11]

These lines echo the image of man below the throne of the sun; the sense of this image, though, is that now the human soul has become its own source of illumination and judgement. However, the problem is that the fall of the last priest does not resolve a central difficulty. Who will intercede for the unseen power? Could it be the poet? This is connected to the very problem of judgement. One has to pretend to a perspective of all-encompassing knowledge of which God was the foundation. Shelley may have swept God away, but he inherits the problem of an overarching standard of judgement to which his sense of Liberty can appeal. Further difficulties follow. The next sentence is conditional: '[o]h that the words . . .' The complaint is that the words one uses to articulate truth and falsity are merely words that do not correspond with the actuality of these states. The hope is that they will be 'stripped of their thin masks' until in their 'nakedness' they 'stand before their Lord' and receive their due; a sentiment that echoes the desire that Liberty provide the perfect order, the fair exchange.

The truth is more disturbing. In the penultimate stanza, the reader encounters the familiar tension. The apostrophe 'come thou!' followed by the acknowledgement that Liberty is 'self-moving' and ultimately does not appear. Shelley is yearning for a kind of apocalypse, a judgement of 'life's ill apportioned lot' in the name of 'Blind Love' and 'Equal Justice' in the name of what is either past or deferred: 'the Fame/Of what has been, the Hope of what will be'.[12] One might expect that this is in the name of Liberty, but it escapes even this summoning. Neither hope nor fame is the name of Liberty. Liberty seems permanently 'disjoined' from these terms. Moreover, its excessiveness remains in the fact that could she be bought, those that have wept blood and tears for her had surely paid her price. We are forced to the conclusion

[11] *Ibid.*, 97.
[12] *Ibid.*, 98.

that Liberty has no price, no name, no equivalent, and yet her voice can still be heard.

This is the final concern of the poet. If Liberty cannot be named, it seems that the disappearance of the poet is at least a prior condition for the calling. This could return to the concerns of *Ozymandias*. To be true to Liberty, Shelley can leave no monument, he must provoke others to act in the name of something that resists representation. Indeed, this is the task of poetry. The poem has already instructed us in this truth. Poetry praises Liberty:

> In songs whose music cannot pass away,
> Though it must flow forever: not unseen
> Before the spirit sighted countenance
> Of Milton thou didst pass, from the sad scene
> Beyond whose night he saw, with a dejected mien.[13]

The name of the poet is something and nothing. Compared with the music of the song itself, the name will be forgotten. It is this forgetful remembering that allows the name of Milton to be linked with Liberty. Liberty can only be named in a kind of erasure. The great voice disappears into its own echoes, the poem ends with an image of death:

> As waves which lately paved his watery way
> Hiss round a drowner's head in their tempestuous play.[14]

It is a conclusion similar in some ways to that in *Ozymandias*. Life disappears into a world that stretches away. When the figure of a man appears, it is to be obliterated, to leave a world that simply carries on meaninglessly. This is precisely the challenge. Shelley has to disappear from the poem to leave it to the reader. The hissing waves are a figure, in the end, of the absence that allows Liberty to be written. Refer back to the earlier image of erasure. Authentic writing is a form of disappearance:

> O that the free would stamp the impious name
> Of KING into the dust! Or write it there,

---

[13] Shelley, n. 3 *supra*, 95.
[14] *Ibid.*, 98.

So that this blot upon the page of fame
Were as a serpents path, which the light air
Erases, and the flat sands close behind.[15]

Sand and water flow throughout this poem, writing and erasing names. Sand recalls the desert of *Ozymandias,* the shifting, infinite, placeless place that buries the icons of empire. But for the name of Shelley to live, it must disappear also.

Act in memory of what has disappeared, but may come again.

It is the law of Liberty, the law of the heart.

Nothing besides remains.

---

[15] *Ibid.,* 96. For an insightful consideration of death and other erasures, see Williams, M., *Euthanasia and the Ethics of Trees: Law and Ethics through Aesthetics The Australian Feminist Law Journal* 10 (1998), 109–25.

Index

Index

www.ingramcontent.com/pod-product-compliance
Lightning Source LLC
Chambersburg PA
CBHW061322220326
41599CB00026B/4994